MARCIA B HORN

Her Family Tree

Alcoholism, Murder, Love, a Tragic Accident, Prison,
Redemption

D1714619

PLATYPUS
PUBLISHING

First published by Platypus Publishing 2024

Copyright © 2024 by Marcia B Horn

First edition

ISBN: 978-1-962133-85-2

Alcoholism, Love, Murder, Addiction,
a Tragic Accident, Redemption

Her Family Tree

Contents

Preface

Hello, my name is Marcia and I am an alcoholic. I want to share my story but I can not tell you who I am without first telling you about my Mother and my Grandmother. I think who I am and the things I've done will make more sense when you know more about them. I was raised the way I was as a result of my grandmother's murder. I received alcoholism through my family tree and I am one of many in the bloodline that suffer this disease. It has affected every fiber of my upbringing, and I never knew about it. This is what it was like, what happened, and what it is like now.

I

Part One: Gladys

Gladys Rae Ours, born January 6, 1935 in Westernport, Maryland was killed in February of 1971 by her husband. She was raised in a gentle Appalachian town in Western Maryland in a wholesome, religious family who were disappointed when she married young. In her life she was a loving, musical, creative and faithful woman who in death, has left a small legacy and a very large family tree.

Gladys

Gladys Rae Ours, Age 15

Westernport, Maryland 1950

I've lived here in these mountains all my life. Through both World Wars and the Depression, my parents kept us in clothes, food and even toys the whole time. Pappy works at the Paper Mill, which is five steps up from the Coal Mine where Joe's family works. I met him at Teen Town on Main Street, we dance, drink soda and talk, well and other things too, I should say. But I know when they find out I'm pregnant, they won't let me stay here. They simply will not accept it, what with all the church events we get involved in and the Mayor and his wife next door being my parent's best friends. My Mother will be mortified.

I'm 15 years old, which is older than most girls in school, though my older sisters both went to college. I know I must drop out and marry Joe, it is the right thing to do. I think we'll be alright, though he doesn't come from much, over the other side of the river. He lives with his parents, brother, aunt and cousin, all of them in a barn! His father can't even read or write, and they don't have a toilet, running water, electricity or a phone. We have a phone.

Oh what will my Mother say? They haven't encouraged this. They took me to Detroit to get me away from him for the summer and what they didn't realize is that he was there too, that's how I ended up this way. But he's so handsome! I do not know another person in this world like him. He likes Hank Williams and Woody Guthrie but I like the new swing and big bands. I was taught to Rumba and Swing, but he didn't have any lessons like that. I learned the piano young, and I know all the church hymns. Come to think of it, I've had a much better go of life than Joe. We're going to change all of that when we get married. They'll see how happy we are and he can get a good job and we'll make it alright.

Gladys Rae Neat (Ours) Age 22

Detroit, 1957

Our wedding was quiet and wasn't long before we came here to Detroit. Bill, Joe's brother, had work at the auto factory and helped Joe get into the union. He goes down to the Union Hall every time he gets laid off and they always send him somewhere. It's not much but he always finds something. He's been back to Maryland for work twice now, but both times we've ended up back here in Detroit. Chrysler has finally picked him up and now we're talking about going to the Delaware plant. I have had enough success taking in ironing at $4 a basket to feed the little ones. He keeps drinking our money away. When he's home, no one can make a sound, which means I rarely get to play the piano anymore. I wouldn't want to wake him anyway, he's nearly destroyed my face the way he beats on me sometimes. It is the alcohol that does it, neither him or Bill can take whiskey. But after a hard night at work he deserves a drink, well that's how he says it.

I can't forgive him for making me give up the baby. I don't know where he gets it into his head that I've been untrue. Sure I've accepted a few pennies from cousin Eddie for the little ones, but that doesn't make a baby! He gets so angry and just starts making things up. I almost believe him myself about the things he says I've done. I have to remind myself it's not him, it's the liquor. He wouldn't hurt me if he wasn't drunk. Our problem is that he keeps getting drunk. I try to keep him quiet and keep it from the kids, and I do not believe they know anything about it. What I can't explain is why their sister was put up for adoption. How does a Mother explain something like that? It is a horrible, horrible thing he's done. He told me this wasn't his baby and took me to a witch doctor in West Virginia for a coat hanger abortion. I refused, ran away terrified for my life and finally he let up but made me swear to put the baby up for adoption and that's what we've done. He is probably insecure about the money and not being able to provide for us, but instead he drinks and starts hitting and blaming me. When I gave birth to baby Judith in the hospital they let me see her and then took her from my arms. I could not get any memento like her footprints or baby blanket but I will never forget her sweet face. A few weeks later the hospital mistakenly sent me her birth certificate. I never told anyone about it, but I keep it hidden as one of my most prized possessions and I hold it and think of her all the time. I know that she went to a good family but I do not know who they are and desperately hope to find her again one day.

Well there is no doubt in any way that this baby isn't his, we have been together now this whole two years since. I do not know what is worse, him being here or him being gone. I doubt Ellen and Craig have spent more than a month in his company. I suppose I'm just upset, pregnancy always gets me emotional. At least there is Regina and Bill, they help with him when he gets out of control. I can't believe the way these men drink, neither of them has the ability to control their temper after whiskey, but then neither can their father and from what I've seen he's the worst of them all.

Gladys Rae Neat (Ours) Age 30

Delaware 1965

After Shelia, our youngest, was born, we left Detroit and Bill & Regina let us move into the Pennsylvania house when they moved. We brought the piano but my love of music has been silenced like many other things in my life. Joe's mother passed away in the shack in West Virginia and his father came to live with us. His father is a specimen much like my Joe, they both drink till they can't see straight. I know now that he has learned this behavior from his father, and that is also where he learned how to treat women. His father, Scott Neat, is one of 11 children and he never went to school but stayed behind to work on the farm. He has struggled with Epilepsy since childhood and that may be why they kept him from school but the result is that he has mountain-man survival skills only useful in depression era

Appalachia, he does not quite fit in with modern society. He has never used an indoor toilet like we have and makes a terrible mess in our bathroom, I won't let the children go in there until I've checked to make sure it is clean enough. The man worked at the coal mine and raised his children in a small barn that some family friends let him stay in, when it was too shabby to keep the mules in any longer. It seems that Scott was the father of cousin Eddie as well, and the family mostly keeps quiet about that. I was raised with fine manners in an upscale neighborhood and his way of life is foreign to me. It does shed light on the affect that upbringing must have had on my husband.

We have been stable in this home over five years now. It didn't take too long for Joe to come up with the money to get us all into our own home in Delaware, once he started at the plant there. It's a much closer drive from where we live now. He keeps busy with work and isn't around with the family much, but when he is, the drinking seems to be worse. He spends many a night at the racetrack.

Every time we go back to Westernport where we are from, he will drop us off for weeks or months to stay with Mam and Pappy. I love the driving there, most of it is through mountains where we stop for picnics along the way, getting fresh spring water for our containers and the car. At the top of Dan Mountain the car always overheats, and there's a lookout where we take the kids and show them the towns from above. You can see where the river splits Westernport, Maryland from Piedmont, West Virginia. When my parents said he was from the wrong side of the tracks they literally meant it. Looking back over the last fifteen years I can see the wisdom of their advice. Sometimes

I wonder who I would be now if I hadn't run away with him. Thank the good Lord my parents have stayed on our side, they covered for me of course, and put it together to look like a love match. I don't believe I knew what love was in those days, so young was I.

Mam is in her cleaning dress, scrubbing the porch when we arrive. To me she is the most sophisticated, well-mannered Christian woman I know. They have sent us gifts and letters through the years and we come here at least once every year. I am grateful the children have these memories, something to cherish the way I do. The smell of the pulp from the paper mill spreads at least fifty miles, and when you look over the side of the mountain it's easy to see where the mill is, all the ground is black and the trees are bare. It was a good job for Pappy and by the time he retired he was a supervisor. He had been in his twenties during the first war and his forties during the second, though he didn't go to the front we were rationed like all other families. My mother knew how to make the littlest things special, she could make brownies from Coco Wheats and candies from day old potatoes. I have always done that with my own children, once I had to use the curtains to make the girls dresses but they never knew we were in need, the way I presented it. I go to the church rummage sale where I pick out dresses with the big skirts and I cut those up to make clothing for our children. I have always been able to sew and all of their doll's clothing is homemade. Ellen and Shelia love the Barbie and Ken dolls, something nice I did for them when they came out at the Newark Five and Dime. I saved my ironing money and brought them to the store to pick one out and Ellen was so overwhelmed by the choices she had the hardest time selecting

8

one. They keep their toys clean and orderly, never a mess has been left in our house for long.

When we get back to Delaware I am starting work at the Diner. Joe will be furious because coal miners have the notion that all waitresses might as well be prostitutes. His mother was a waitress and I have heard that she also did that as well, although it may all be rumor, I'll never know the truth. These men have the strangest ideas. I have been quietly making plans to leave him, Regina says she will help me get away from him and maybe with getting a car to use. I have been learning to drive and finally got my license last year. Oh that doesn't mean I can make the 9 hour drive to Westernport! No, Joe has always been the driver and he's good with cars. Always has been. But I did take the children out in the car once I will never forget, they opened up a MacDonald's restaurant in town and sell hamburgers for fifteen cents. I took the car while he was asleep and the four of us drove over to see what it was all about. Don't you know there was trash blowing all over the road? They sell sandwiches in paper to take along with you, no plates or indoor seating. We all thought it was marvelous.

Gladys Rae Neat (Ours) Age 31

Delaware 1966

Regina got us out during the night while Joe was at work, and with the money from my parents I was able to get us this little trailer to live in. I was nervous the entire trip back, hiding what they gave me. Working at the diner I eventually had enough to know I could leave safely. Of course, safety is relative when Joe shows up angry and drunk, shaking the trailer and beating on it from outside. I turn up the radio and lock the doors, eventually he leaves. He is sore but I know we are all better off split up like this. He would not give us the children's toys, clothing or even the piano after we left, I thought he would go easy on them but he seems to be taking it out on them, too. We are officially divorced and I have been working at the other diner in town for a few months already. I decided to change jobs so that Joe would not know where I was all the time. I met Len there.

Len wants to marry me, he promised to buy me a piano, he says we can have a vacuum cleaner and new dishes. He has a good job with the city and comes to the diner for breakfast every day. He's older, 50 at least, but he's refined and gentlemanly. He says he will take care of me and the kids and I won't have to work, which does sound nice. Then I can attend church on Sundays again and not feel embarrassed for being unwed.

Well I may as well admit it, I'm going to marry Len because now I'm pregnant again and we'd better get married before I start to show. I know we'll be fine with him, he is good to me. Charming, funny, quick witted ... I think I will finally have a chance at happiness.

Gladys Rae Hill (Ours)

Rock Hill South Carolina, 1969

This man is a monster! He is moving us again because he lost another city job here, drunk again in the company car. How did I not know he was a drinker too? He makes Joe look like the good one, of course there will be no help from that quarter. Ellen and Craig both ran away in Delaware, and every time I get them back he throws them out. I don't know what to do. He's mean to the baby and my little Shelia. He hurt Ellen so bad one night she walked right out the front door with a bloody nose and two black eyes. Bill came for her and thank the Lord she had somewhere to go for a little while. The problem there is of course Joe, and not having a mother to take care of her she was living with Joe, Bill, their father and my boy Craig. I don't think one person goes to the grocery store or cooks in that house. No, she had to come back with us again and I don't think this boyfriend of hers is going to leave her here for long. No, I certainly wouldn't if I was him. Steve is a nice young man from a good family in Delaware, she may be better off if she marries him.

Len's mother is here for another week and every time she comes into town he gets worse. She's terrible on me, I can't seem to do anything right. From my cooking and cleaning skills to the way I treat him, nothing is good enough. When I saw her slap Shelia I did not know what to do, I let her know it was unacceptable and paid dearly for that comment when Len found out. He said he would be good to us, but he started hitting me right after little Sharon was born. Oh Lord preserve me. We moved here to South Carolina because he lost the job in Delaware when he wrecked the company truck drunk. Now he's lost this job too, after repeatedly being counseled for his drinking he was passed out on the side of the road during the work day. He drinks his vodka before he gets out of bed, he drinks it all day on the job and then goes to the bar after work. I have to keep dinner hot and wait to feed everyone together because Len insists we all eat together at the table as a family. When he shows up at seven or eight o'clock at night to a cold meal, he gets angry and starts shouting and hitting whoever he sees first. He's broken so many of the nice dishes he got me for our wedding. He finds something wrong with every single thing I do, and threatens to hurt me whenever he's not hurting me.

This level of violence is something I've never seen before. I have never even heard of anything like this. Not as if women would tell it, but at church I don't see bruised women and I cover it well with makeup and I won't tell anyone. I am mortified at the thought of anyone finding out, although Len's mother and sister obviously know, and my children, and now they are getting old enough to where their friends are starting to figure it out. The neighbors can hear him. They've seen him passed out in the front yard and I always have to try to cover for him. Well, now we're moving anyway so maybe we can have a fresh start. He says he will change, he says he's sorry and he wants a clean slate and of course it is my duty to forgive him. I have to remind myself it is not him, it's the liquor. When he isn't drinking he is charming and funny. The problem with Len is that he gets mean when he's drinking, and he's always drinking.

Gladys Rae Hill (Ours) Age 36

Charlotte, North Carolina, February 1971

I've left him. This is the scariest thing I've ever done! He says he'll kill me and he begs me to come back home, what exactly does he expect me to believe? Will he kill me or does he want me back? I am terrified of what he'll do. I started going to Al-Anon here in Charlotte, where I met a group of women with similar problems. I heard about the group at church, where some of the women also attend. Betty has been letting us stay, Sharon and me. February is cold in Westernport but I still found a way to send Shelia there and with Pappy gone now, my Mam is happy to have her. I have to get some things from the house, when we ran we got out with just the shirts on our back and nothing else. Here's my big problem, when I took Len for custody of Sharon they put me on the stand and asked me all sorts of questions. I told them he scares me and the judge told Len he wasn't supposed to hurt me if I came back to get some things from the house. They asked me how many children I have and I said four. I was so nervous I suppose I didn't mention Judith, the baby Joe made me put up for adoption. It's not as if I have any clue where she is or if she's even alive, but Len is threatening me that I've lied on the stand and he thinks to force me to come back to him by terrorizing me. All I need is the birth certificate from the dresser, it's there in the bedroom and if I can get that back I can keep it quiet and should be able to get Sharon away. We will go back to Westernport and stay for a while, my boy Craig says he's coming down to take us. Ellen and Steve are married now, thank the good Lord and hopefully she has a healthy baby soon and I want more than anything to be there to help her with this pregnancy.

Betty from Al-Anon is going to follow me in her car to the house where I can pick up some things. It is the best plan I have at this point, her husband can't come, he's at work, and has forbidden her to go inside with me. She will wait in her car across the street. I called the police department this morning and asked for an escort, I'm afraid of him! They know Len at the police department, he's been causing trouble since we got here. What did they tell me? "Lady, we don't DO that." So I have to go with my plan and get in there and see what belongings I can retrieve, including those adoption papers. I need all the kid's birth certificates, their medical and school records, family photos, clothing, I have nothing. I've heard Len's mother Ida is in town, he must have called her when I left but I just hope she isn't at the house when I get there, and he better be at work like he's supposed to. Sharon is safe with my Al-anon network while I go get these things. Lord preserve me.

I'm in the house, Ida is here and she's yelling insults as if I've personally attacked her. She knows what her son is like! How can a woman support the man in this case? Relative or no, it is wrong the way he treats me. I have to hurry, I think she's called his work. I have all the clothes out in my car and I just need the paperwork now. OH NO is that his car coming in the driveway?

II

Part Two: Ellen

Ellen was the daughter of Gladys, raised in the tumult of broken homes and secrets, she was the second child of Gladys and Joe Neat. Her mother was killed when Ellen was only 17, already married with a child on the way. We meet her at this period of her life, after she gets the call about her mother's murder, as she drives south to try to gain custody of her 3 year old sister, still in the killer's hands.

Ellen

Ellen, Age 17

Delaware, 1971

S teve's driving us to North Carolina. We heard from the police this afternoon that my Mother was shot in the bedroom, twice. I thought it was a prank from Len and I hung up the phone, then when they called back Steve took down the information. Witnesses reported Len came home while she was there getting some things, he went in and caught her, then he left and she never came out. It was Betty from Al-anon, she's got Sharon and we have got to get to her. I keep going in and out of a panic. Steve is good with me, after all I'm six months pregnant right now and a drive down the East Coast is the last thing I need, I've been so sick in the mornings. My Mother was going to come and stay with us, help with the baby. I can't believe she's gone. Everyone said he would kill her one day, including her. Now he's really done it, I hope they catch him! We hardly know anything at this point, just that we need to get there and get to Sharon. Steve and I adore that little girl, she is beautiful, a sweet and funny little thing. She likes to sit on

Steve's chest and tug on his beard. Len was never nice to her, the last time I saw him with her he was being mean again, like usual. He would stuff food in her mouth till she gagged, crying all the while, pushing her in the face and making her eat the food he paid for. Everything was money to him, and he let Mom know just how expensive we were to support.

My Mother called me last night and told me how happy and free she was feeling. She had just come from an Al-Anon meeting at church and was in such a great mood. She told me her plan for this morning, and that she had Judith's birth certificate pinned together with some quilting materials, hidden in the top drawer of Sharon's dresser, that she needed to get from Len's house. She was planning to borrow a car from a friend, leave Sharon with another friend, and also have someone meet her near the house. She was excited about the Lord working in her life and was positive He had a plan for her future. She said she did not know where God would take her next but that she was so alive with His spirit she felt she could accomplish anything. Here she was thinking God was about to do something for her, and then He took her home to be with Him in Heaven.

Maybe she is still alive, maybe she survives this and they took her to the hospital after they called us. She might live. I know they said she wasn't alive when they found her but maybe they were wrong? We might get there and find that she's in the hospital recovering, and not the morgue. We could just take her home with us, I'd care for her, I'm sure I could help her heal and we can all have a fresh start. We'll find room for Sharon, and her, it can work I know it can.

What if Len finds us? If he comes after us, too? My word, is he mean. He did not start out that way, I remember the trailer and him treating my Mother like a princess. He brought us all gifts, had a nice car, he was a Civil Engineer for the city of Newark in those days. He was funny and charismatic. He never told my Mother he was married before her, and no one knows how his first wife died. She did not know about his son or his other step children from his second wife, either. She was upset about the lying, from the very beginning he pulled the wool over our eyes. I can remember walking to school from the house we all lived in, in Delaware. I had friends in the neighborhood, in fact it was there where I went when I ran away. That night is seared into my memory, I can't get the images out of my head no matter how I try to forget about it. I was in the bathroom trimming my hair and he came in and started calling me names. He said I was a whore and only cared about my looks, I was thirteen! He took the scissors from my hand and cut my beautiful long hair right to the scalp down the center of my head before taking those scissors and beating me in the face with them. He had me on the ground crying, holding the pointed end of the scissors inches above my eye, screaming, salivating, the stench of vodka coming out of his pores. He banged my head in the doorway, clenching my hair and slamming me into the floor. What I don't recall is how I got away from him, did my Mother stop him? There was never anything she could do to stop him, and it usually made things worse. She couldn't get him off of Craig, Shelia, Sharon or me. He would get so angry. I've never seen anything like it, almost as if he was possessed by the Devil. That night when he was at the dinner table being mean to Sharon, I waved to Shelia to try to get her to come with me but she was too scared. She sat on the couch watching the Wizard of Oz, terrified to move or make a sound. I think that is why she's always been so quiet. So I walked right out the front door with my bag but then I started running and when I got to my friend's house her Mother took me right in. I thought I would be able to call someone, my Dad or Uncle or maybe Aunt Regina, but the house was dark, and I realized they didn't have electricity! My friend didn't have a phone. But they found some change for me and her mother's boyfriend walked me out into the dark and showed me the path through the fields where I could run through to a laundromat a few miles down. I called Dad and my Uncle Bill came for me.

Now we are passing one of the picnic areas we always used to stop at going to Westernport with my Mother and Father. We went up there every year, drove through the mountains and would stop along the way to let the car cool down, we would collect our water at the spring and she always had a picnic basket packed for us kids. We knew when we were getting close to their hometown because you could smell the paper mill before you saw it. She was a great Mother. She knew how to make every little thing special, the smallest cake she would split into pieces and serve with a story or a song. She made our dolls and their clothes, created toys out of washrags. I don't really understand why my Mother left my Father, but I remember Aunt Regina picking us up in the middle of the night while he was at work and taking us away. I never saw very much of my Father growing up, he was never home. He's helped where he could after their divorce but he'll never forgive my Mother for leaving. He's with Grandad Neat and Bill now, still in our old Delaware house. I don't see much of him now, either. I tried living with them to get away from Len but had to go back to Mother's because I did not have anywhere to rest, or food to eat.

Shelia is in Westernport, my Mother told me she was sending her up there before she left. Len couldn't be trusted, and any day with him was one of walking on eggshells. No-one said a word, the air was so heavy with the anticipation of setting him off. When is he going to break next, who is he going after tonight? It was a horror. I remember learning to drive with him, I was driving the car, we were in South Carolina, and he started laughing this hideous, malicious sound, and he pressed his leg on top of mine and stomped the gas pedal all the way to the floor, I could hardly control the vehicle at top speed like that and I screamed and screamed and he just kept laughing. I was terrified, almost all the time before Steve came down and got me. He picked me up one day and took me to Delaware to live with him and his family and we got married. Then we bought a house a few streets over from his parents. Oh, they are an interesting bunch! My Steve is six foot three, great big arms and great big chest, he looks a little like Elvis Presley only with a fuller, black beard. He always has his hair combed and lifts weights and rides his motorcycle and he loves cars. He does construction work on the side and works at the Penn Jersey store full time, and we are making it just fine, until this happened.

I am getting my High School diploma at Grove's Night School in Newark now, after changing between ten different schools in Jr and Sr high and moving the way we did there was no chance at finishing any other way. As soon as I have all my courses complete I'll start the nursing program, they have an accelerated degree at the community college and I can do some of my labs on my own time, I should be able to do that with the baby. I think I fell pregnant last year when my Pappy Ours passed away, it was so hard on Mam Ours. The nicest people you ever will meet, they took as good care of us as my Mother ever did. I have such beautiful memories of Westernport, and the friends we made in the neighborhood. Whenever we visited when I was a child we always went to church with Mam and Pap, he would go early and start the stove to heat the church and Mam was always involved in the Sunday School and after church events. Sometimes she would have a Payday candy bar saved for my Mother, who always split it up for all of us to share, it was her favorite. We only went to the Neat's shack a few times. They lived in an old barn on the Evan's property where they used to keep the cow and mules in the 1930s, converted it to living space where Dad was raised with his parents, brother, aunt and cousin. They had a dirt floor, a water pump outside and used an outhouse for a bathroom and bathed outside. They slept on benches cut into the walls on either side of the room and never did have electricity but ran a long extension cord all the way up the mountain from the Evan's house to the shack. Granddad is absolutely unique, after Mommom Maddie died he came to live with us and he could smell a rattlesnake outside from the dinner table! He would get up during our meal sometimes and storm out there to kill a snake by the blackberry bushes, then come back and finish dinner as if nothing ever happened. Right in the middle of supper. He is an illiterate, and he has seizures, his siblings, including his twin brother, all went and had fine lives. It doesn't sound like he was a very nice man to his family, and I wonder sometimes if that is where my Father gets his behavior.

I know I am all over the place right now, remembering things in order of how they occur to me during this drive. Anything is better than thinking about my Mother's last few moments, escaping from Len, going for custody of Sharon, the Al-anon ladies, the fighting and the hiding, she must have been terrified. She was always scared, what a terrible way to live. I am so lucky I found Steve. I don't think I realized my family was unusual until I met his. Now there is a good group of people. His parents always want to help, I know they'll be good with the baby. His Father went into teaching after WW2 and he has a fine reputation, he's very charismatic, and plays the organ at church. His Mother Ruth brings over food all the time, I knew Steve's sister and that is how we met. Someone said I think men with beards are handsome! She introduced us after that.

Now we are getting into Charlotte, we will go to Betty's from Al-anon first and see what she's found out. It's after two in the morning right now, but I doubt anyone is asleep.

Sharon is not here! Betty says they came late at night and got her, put her into foster care because Len's mother and sister are trying to take her. They do not want her to get into his family's hands, they are terrible people. Mean, angry, violent, all of them.

Ellen, Age 18

Newark, Delaware, 1972

We couldn't get Sharon. We stayed in Charlotte for weeks, fighting for her. Len got my Mother's life insurance policy money and bailed out of jail within the month, then he showed up at Sharon's custody hearing and demanded she gets put with his family. What world do we live in here!? As her parent, he apparently had more say than us. He claimed he was innocent

23

until proven guilty. We fought the entire year and then when her custody hearing finally came, the social worker missed it and didn't tell us the date. She got sick, turned her report in late. This has to be undone somehow. Len was charged with murder and his first trial had a hung jury, 11 members of the jury found him guilty right away and there was 1 person holding out, who could possibly understand why. I'll never know, but he finally plead guilty to manslaughter. His mother took the stand and told all kinds of lies, but it was she who hid the murder weapon in a gallon of ice cream from the police! These people are evil. It is bad enough that Ida instigated so many fights between my Mother and Len, but then to take the stand and lie and faint and cause a scene, she's a terrible person. How will Sharon ever survive?

I couldn't go into her funeral, she is buried in Westernport next to her Pap. I just did not want the image in my head. All our family and friends were there, it was a big deal in Westernport and all over the papers from North Carolina to West Virginia. I couldn't go to the trial, my brother Craig took Shelia, he was able to scrape some money together and go down from Newark. He's told me all about it. Len plead guilty to manslaughter and got 15-20 years in the North Carolina state prison. I hope he never makes it out. My Mam is so upset about everything, she said she would answer the door with a pot of boiling water if he ever came to her house. She is not one to get angry, but this has devastated her, and our entire family. There is nowhere for Shelia to go, my Father doesn't want her but I fear that's where she will end up anyway. She's only 15 now and the courts insist on her being with a parent, not us. What a mess. A terrible, terrible mess. How will any of us survive it? Thank God for Steve and his family, they have been wonderful with baby Sarah.

Ellen, Age 27

Newark, Delaware, 1980

I am pregnant with my 4th child, I just got hired at the Christiana Hospital where they finally lifted the hiring freeze on nurses. I have been working at St Frances for a couple of years now but what I really want is to get into the Labor & Delivery department and Christiana has the best birthing center. All three of my children were born at Wilmington General of course, that's our family hospital and Shelia has had both her children there. Steve and I are settled into our lives, the last decade is full of fond memories. We haven't become rich, no we have found a way to make due with what we've had and support all three children, though this one will be our last, we've decided on that. We didn't plan on having more than two! I think the kids have fun, though Steve's parents finally finished the house on their property in Pennsylvania we still see quite a bit of them. Charlie, Steve's father, can be seen in the tree out front with Sarah and Chuckie, climbing as high as he can. We usually spend the weekend playing cards with our friends and neighbors downstairs, or volleyball when the weather is nice. My Steve is a little bit competitive and I've caught him hosing down the ground of the opponent's side of the yard where we play volleyball. He's a big kid! I can't say he's too helpful with the cooking, cleaning or childcare, but he's had work at Gore for years now and he loves these children. Any time we go to a pool, he does a cannonball or belly flop off the diving board. He's taught them all to swim, Shelia and I dress them in the cutest outfits and when we had

Sarah I was so young sometimes I felt as if I was dressing up a little doll baby. She is the apple of her daddy's eye, and Steve is so proud to have two 'good looking' sons. Yes, we do alright.

The 1970's were a difficult time for the Ours family, first my grandfather passed away in 1970. After my own Mother was killed in '71 her sister Louise passed away in '73. My Grandmother made it two more years and died of pneumonia the day my first son was born. It is strange that I became pregnant with my daughter when grandad died then had my son as my grandmother died. I am not superstitious though, I am a Christian, but I believe if God sends us signs, those would be two.

I have tried to come to terms with my Mother's death through the years, but all we can do is just not talk about it and her name and her story have been silenced. It is just too painful. The latest news about Len came through this week, we heard that he got out of prison a few years ago on good behavior, and he has recently died in a car accident. Some say it was suicide, there is speculation he may have been run off the road, and he was certainly drunk when he drove off the bridge. I never was able to get Sharon back from that family. I send her a gift every Christmas and I write all the time, since I've never heard back I suppose she may not be getting my letters from Len's sister. Shelia and I have both prayed for her every single day since all of that happened. I'll see her again someday, I know I will.

Ellen, Age 33

Newark, Delaware, 1986

After Marcia was born we got pregnant one last time... twins! We have children everywhere! Steve and I wash the children in an assembly line – I hand a baby in to him in the shower and he hands one out. Right now Sarah is 15, Chuckie is 11, Brian is 7, Marcia is 5 and the twins are 3. Steve is building us a bigger house, we plan on moving to Pennsylvania closer to his parents, as soon as we can. I know I've already said thank God for those people, but thank God for those people! Through the years they have really helped out with the kids, so has my sister Shelia. My brother Craig has been on & off the scene through the years, always shows up when Steve needs a hand with something. I have not seen much of my own Father, of course he's met all of the children but we aren't close. He's remarried now to a very kind woman and I do believe she's never seen him drink. He seems to have changed completely and I believe she has been his redemption.

There have been many interesting events this last couple of years, probably the most exciting is Judith. Yes, I found her. I hired a private investigator to see if they could locate my sister, the baby my father made my mother give up for adoption, saying she wasn't his. She was in Louisiana, raised by a very loving family and happily married with two kids of her own. We stay in touch and visit whenever we can, the newspapers covered our reunion. The best is that she looks just like us, and so do her children! She is a Neat, through and through. She is beautiful, active in the church and plays piano and sings like an angel, she was happy to hear that her biological mother also loved music. We told her the story. My Father did eventually come around and admit he may have been wrong about it. What a shame, though at least she seems to have had a better life than what we did growing up. I try not to ever think of the bad and I have been very good at keeping the darker images of the past from my children. They are in a Christian school, they haven't been exposed to any alcohol or drinking, and they do not know about my mother. Our four girls all wear dresses and I get each child a new pair of saddle shoes every year. We do have most of what we need in this family, God has provided for me in my adult life and I give praise and tithe every Sunday at church.

I have a babysitter I use from the neighborhood, a teen girl who comes and helps with the kids while I am at work. My eldest girls took piano lessons from my best friend, Lynette, who lives down the street. Steve and I spend time with her and her husband sometimes. They have a pool and enjoy letting the kids swim, with just one daughter of their own, our family can fill the silence pretty quickly. Yes, we have a good time with them. Our relationships grow and change as our family grows. After the Vietnam war ended in the 70s, many of our friendships changed. Steve was too heavy to go to war, even though he did register and tried to do his duty. When the men came back they were different, and yes it did change some of our relationships I must say.

Perhaps the biggest surprise of all was when we found out that Steve was adopted. It came as a surprise one day when his sister Esther was helping clean out the attic at his parents, now formally 'Grandmom and Poppop,' on their farm in Pennsyl-

28

vania. Oh they have a beautiful property, horses and acres of land with a pond in Nottingham. They are both retired now and live a wholesome life, very involved with their church. As I said, it came as a big surprise when Esther ran across adoption paperwork last year and it had my husband as born to a Cathleen Hornberger in Philadelphia 1948. I used the same agency and located her, and would you believe it she was at least 600 lbs! Now, Steve has always been overweight and very tall, but his parents and sister are all much smaller people, and he doesn't really look like any of them but we never questioned it. What a secret!! Now we know that obesity is in his bloodline and will have to watch out for it. She had one other child who is also very heavy set, and she is a peculiar woman. She said she was very in love with Steve's biological father, but they were unwed and her father refused to accept the pregnancy and sent her away, forcing her to give up her first child. She was thrilled to finally see him again. We've been to New York where she lives and had her out once to visit. She immediately went to the piano and played beautiful, stunning melodies all by ear. It is interesting to see because my 5 year old Marcia is already showing that she plays the piano by ear and now we see where it comes from.

Finally and also quite exciting is the news about Sharon. She is okay. We heard from her recently that she is 20 now and married to a young man in Vermont. We have been able to see her. It is sad to have confirmed that she did not have a happy life with Len's sister, as everyone feared. She seems to hold no resentment though, which is a single testament to my Mother's personality, she turned out to be loving and kind, against all odds. I found out that she always received a gift at Christmas that she knew was from me, though it was never labeled and the cards and letters were never given to her. She said that she knew her biological mother had passed away but she never knew any more about it, and that she remembered her even though she was only four at the time her mother was murdered. She had been brought to visit Len in prison as a girl, and later before he died she did not live with him but spent holidays with him. Interestingly, she says he kept a photo of Gladys in his home in Vermont, along with quite a lot of vodka.

Ellen, Age 39

Oxford, Pennsylvania, 1992

We live in this enormous, beautiful house in Oxford that Steve built, on a gorgeous property with acres of land, woods, a barn, silo, pond and a swimming pool. We have a beach house in Bethany Beach, Delaware and have been spending family summers there for years now. Shelia, her husband and her four kids come down and we have had many fun and happy years there. My oldest, Sarah, is married, happily, I am glad to say, and the youngest girls adore her husband. Chuck, my oldest son, is on the high school football team and big like his father, he is very popular and we have him in the local public school so he can play sports. The four youngest are in a Mennonite school and we all are very involved in the Presbyterian church that we are members of in Oxford. I teach Sunday School and we have youth group on Wednesdays. There has never been any alcohol in this house, I am glad to say, and though I spend a lot of hours at the hospital working the night shift in Labor & Delivery, I know the children are provided for. I don't believe any of them suspect anything about our marriage, even though

I have not slept in the same bedroom with Steve since 1988. I am not happy to admit this but I've known about my husband's cheating for years. Oh it isn't that we argue or fight, we just don't love each other. I suspect at some point I may not be able to hide it from the kids forever and have started looking into divorce. It is the last thing I would want for my children but I am afraid they will find out where their father goes when we are at the beach, or on the nights when he comes home after 2am. I don't think he's drinking, in fact I know he isn't and it is such a silent issue with him going to those clubs that I would never know how to address it with the children. It is better if we just quietly separate and move on when it can be arranged.

I've been steadily working at the hospital in Delaware all along. I now have seniority in the department and have helped deliver babies of many of our family friends. Steve's parents take the kids once a week when the cleaning lady comes, and she helps keep the house in order. Cooking and cleaning never became his strong suit, and I've found a way to make due. I feel as if I am always busy, and if I sit down to rest there is something to get done that I'm missing. In a way I regret Sarah having to help so much, she was always looking after the younger ones and I know she will be a great mother when she has children of her own. The girls always want to go to her house, and she moved very close to Grandmom and Poppop's in Nottingham, so it has been working out for them to see her.

I've done the best I could with what I've had. I hope my children grow up knowing that all I have sheltered them from was for their own protection. I don't want them to know any of the violence I suffered as a child, or the having to go without all the time like I did. They have always had a roof over their head, good clothes, shoes and toys, the best dance and music lessons I could find, and as much opportunity as their father and I had to offer. I believe we are training them up to be good people.

Ellen, Age 46

Elkton, Maryland, 1999

Marcia is graduating from the Mennonite high school this year, Brian has already graduated and moved out into the world, along with Chuck. It is just Marcia and the twins and I now, and they are all in boarding school. I've had a difficult time as a single parent. When I left Steve I had one job three teenagers and two pre-teens and we moved here to this house. We kept it from the kids until moving day. Steve and I lived in the Oxford house together, divorced, for over a month. I thought we would move and start fresh, not have to announce it at church. When we moved here the kids started asking where Dad was going to sleep, since the master bedroom had only a small twin bed. That is when I sat them all down in the new family room and told them. It was after we had moved everything in and Steve had left with the moving truck, of course he helped us get settled first. This house had everything we needed at the time and since he would not help with child support I had to make difficult decisions about using the heat or air conditioning and buying food. I had to stop the dance and music lessons and put the kids in public school. Well, it didn't go so well because try though I did to keep the children away from alcohol, they all found it when we moved here. No, not all at once but eventually I did need to deal with teenagers drinking and throwing pool parties here while I was at work. I have to work the night shift, the extra $2 an hour is essential if I am going to be able to get by. I appealed to the Mennonite high school which is a boarding school in Lancaster, and they agreed to take all the kids on scholarship. Not that they were appreciative of it, and I wouldn't have expected them to understand, but Marcia got herself thrown out after her first year back. She let the frogs go from the Science lab so they would not be dissected – that child is a vegetarian and really knows how to ruin a good family dinner. I knew I couldn't keep them in public schools, they were exposed to all types of sin. I worry for their souls. I tried to find them a father figure, I am not proud of it because none of the men I introduced were accepted by any of the kids, no matter how hard they tried to be kind to them the kids rejected every suitor. Once the girls egged a man's car in my own driveway. I gave up. I remain a member of this over 40's singles group at the beach and they basically took me in on scholarship. I never had any money to take the kids anywhere after the divorce and these people helped me get them to the beach a few times, they always found a place for us to stay.

Teenagers are complicated, my kids have struggled with things I never intended to expose them to. I underestimated the affect my divorce would have on them. I stay so busy I hardly have time to stop and listen, but I do love them all so very much. Sarah has stepped in from time to time, helping with the girls, and so has my sister Shelia, thank God for her she's everyone's favorite aunt! My friend Lynette has helped me with the kids these last few years and always stayed in touch, though she is divorced now, too. Steve provides for the children at his own convenience, he remarried and they live with his parents, after building in an apartment to their house in Pennsylvania. He usually drives the kids where they need to go and has been doing so for years. I stopped asking him for any money, and try to graciously accept anything he decides to give them. It is a shame though, here they are going without when that is exactly what I was trying to avoid. Still, I won't say a bad word about him and they have no idea I'm struggling financially and that their own father is to blame. He hasn't been as kind on my account, and spent time trying to turn the kids against me. I admit, I've battled with suicidal temptations, wondering if the children would be better off without me. I have struggled to provide and create good memories during these years.

I've taken the kids to Westernport now that they are older, shown them where their family is from and we did go and visit my Mother's grave. I haven't told them much about her, just a few details here and there but they do not understand how hard I've fought to win them a good life. They'll never know what I've overcome. All I can do is my best, and pray.

Ellen, Age 50

Baltimore, Maryland, 2003

When I got the call about Marcia's accident I was at work, it was the middle of the night, and I had a meltdown immediately. I did not know what to do, my coworkers helped me get my things and go home, and by morning all of my friends at the beach knew what she had done. They helped me get an attorney, and figure out how to put my house up to bail her out. Now we are in Baltimore City, because when she was given parole it turned into work release as long as she had somewhere to go within Baltimore City limits. In Ocean City, Maryland where the accident happened, she was a monster and a killer, they portrayed her as a hardened criminal when really she was just 20 and barely knew her own identity yet in life. Here in Baltimore, the prison system sees her as the least of their problems and have offered to let her out early as long as she has an address here in the city. It took time but I managed to sell the house, store my things at my son's place in Newark and find a rental here in Canton. Ironically, the landlord is someone who is sober over 10 years in Alcoholics Anonymous, and he's helping her get connected as she has to attend meetings as part of her punishment.

We held a party for her when she got out of prison, celebrating all the holidays she missed. She sat there sweating in stunned silence. Her brother gave her a keyboard which she plays all the time, she has a guitar and I hear her singing sometimes, sad, eerie songs she's written. The whole family came to the party, even her father, my stepmother, most of her siblings and many cousins.

I take Marcia to report to her parole officer in the city, it is in the worst part of town and honestly I am afraid to wait in the car or get out of it when she goes into the building. Since she is technically still incarcerated and on home detention, every minute out of the house is counted and a few times we've been lost and had to answer to police when we got home, she wears an ankle monitor that needs to be within range of the box in her bedroom. When we are in the car she shakes and jolts all over the seat, she is terrified of getting into another accident. The home detention is so strict that officers come to the house and handcuff her to the furniture and rifle through all of our things, throwing stuff everywhere and yelling in her face, they come and search her all the time at random, even aside from the weekly check-ins. I see how people can get trapped in the system and end up back in prison, because these stipulations are nearly impossible to adhere to, even with both of us focused on compliance. Now she needs to get a job because she is supposed to be on work release, but is not allowed to leave the house to fill out applications. I see her calling through the phone book trying to explain that in order to fill out an application, the business owner needs to send her home detention monitor a fax with signed statements.

She tried to kill herself when it happened. She had been living in California and I was busy making arrangements with Chuck for his wedding. He married a lovely young woman and does well for himself now. Brian was coming home from Alaska for the wedding and we were all planning to attend the twins graduation from the Mennonite school in Lancaster. It was Memorial Day weekend in 2001. The excitement of upcoming events was overshadowed when we found out what happened in Ocean City. I hadn't seen Marcia yet, she was home from California only minutes before she got into her car at her Father's house and went to the beach to see her friends. She should have just stayed with the family, I don't understand why she went when we had all these plans. Her trip home was only supposed to be for two weeks. As soon as I heard about it I started calling the hospital where the young man she hit was taken. His family was very angry, and hateful to me on the phone when I was heartbroken as well. They became known as the victim's family in our conversations. Mother's Against Drunk Drivers immediately took up his case and surrounded their family at the hospital and throughout the trials. We would walk through a mob of angry, hateful people with signs who were shouting things like 'monster!' and 'killer!' every time we went in or out of the building during her trial. MADD filled the courtroom and treated us all as if we were part of it. Where is the group for mothers of drunk drivers? I was and still am desperate for help, I have no idea how to deal with this and I am shattered to have to see the pain in my daughters eyes, knowing what she has to live with. I tried to keep alcohol out of my children's lives, tried in vain to protect and shelter them all. I do not know how to help anyone right now, I tried to talk to the victim's mother but she does not speak English and the translator says that she is very angry with me. Marcia wrote letters and tried to apologize, and MADD suggested they take out a restraining order on my girl. They will never forgive her, and she will never forgive herself. We had to have family members stay with her at my house between trials, before she went to prison. We were all afraid she would try to kill herself and it was a battle we fought hard to get through. I am still not sure we're out of the woods. I hate to say it but how can someone live with that on their conscience?

The young man she hit was 23, he was in the road and also intoxicated, it was after 2:00am and the bars had all just let out so there was a crowd and it was raining that night. Marcia does not remember anything and I wonder if she was drugged by someone at the bar. I have wondered if she was even the driver. There were people driving in front of her that almost hit him, and all of the witness statements conflict. There is no good part of this story, she snuck into a bar at the beach and was grossly drunk when she left the bar, driving drunk in the bus lane she hit this young man who was apparently hailing a cab in the road and then she drove off. The police found her in a parking lot 7 blocks away from the scene of the accident. She was given a 10 year sentence for Vehicular Homicide while Intoxicated, Leaving the Scene of an Accident, Leaving a Person Dead at the Scene of an Accident, DUI and DWI. In the end she will have served 2.5 years on 5, and if she messes up any little thing during this home detention or parole, she goes back for the whole 10 years. She went to the penitentiary after she was sentenced, and we all thought she would be gone for 10 years. What a sad end to 2 young lives. She may be physically living, but when I see her eyes she does not look that way. I do not know how to help her, she goes to counseling with the minister of a church on our street here in Baltimore, maybe she can help her. All I can do is move forward, keep putting one foot in front of the other, and pray.

My drive to work is much longer from Baltimore but I am still at the same hospital. None of the other kids live with us here, they were all out of the house by the time I moved. Now the twins are settling down, Nicki is married with a baby on the way and Megan is in love. Brian returned to Alaska and Sarah and Chuck are both married. Through Marcia's incarceration I became friendly with Steve again, I can't say that we are friends now but we have had to stay in touch to make sure she has visitors. He drove to the penitentiary and took other family members to see her, the entire time she was behind bars and she was transferred three times. It has been a search to keep up with her placement but we managed to figure it out. I am not accustomed to city life and it has been hard for both of us to navigate living like this. Everything has changed and I just try to keep going, it is all I know.

Ellen, Age 58

Baltimore, Maryland, 2011

These last 8 years have been very full, as my children grow up and move about the country, having children of their own. There have been more marriages, divorces, losses and wins as I try to support them from afar. Being a mother is lifelong, and though I did not get to grow older with my own Mother for comfort and guidance, I try to be there for my own children as much as I can. Marcia is asleep on the couch, she is fresh out of rehab and very sick. Drug sick, not health sick. After she got off of home detention in 2004 she left Baltimore, transferred her parole to the edge of DC and went back to college. I was proud of her for a while there, she graduated with a BFA and a 4.0, started modeling, traveling the world and was engaged. I was impressed with the types of friends she had made, spending time with doctors, lawyers and entrepreneurs, but then she just started to spiral. I don't know when her drinking took over but by the time she came back to Baltimore in 2009 she was a full blown alcoholic and had not a penny or prospect to her name. She bounced around from small rentals to staying with friends and family members, even rented an apartment from me briefly. I was able to buy a house in Fell's Point later in 2004, it is a large rowhome split into 4 apartments and I live on the first floor, and rent the other 3 units. I stayed here all this time, still working at the same hospital in Delaware. Now I have much seniority on the floor and an ideal schedule, and have made it work but I do get so tired of all the back and forth. It was difficult to keep track of Marcia when she hit rock bottom, the family pulled together again to keep an eye on her but she was running around faster than some of us could keep up with. I am not sure what all kinds of drugs and pills she was taking, on top of all the drinking, but she eventually came to a place where she thought going to rehab was a good idea. We had come up with a place in Pennsylvania near her father's house that would take her, I helped her get government health insurance because by the end there she was unemployed and unemployable. When she agreed to go to rehab, Chuck had a bag packed for her and her father was ready to drive her there. She was living with Chuck and frankly I think she scared him, she had wrecked another car and we were all afraid she would kill someone else. How much worse did it need to get for her to finally learn her lesson? When an alcoholic hits rock bottom they usually keep going lower and lower until they die, and none of us could handle that. We may not see each other every day in our family but when something urgently comes up like this, we pull together, and that is exactly what we did.

So there she is, on the couch, she is an odd shade of blueish green and she is sick to her stomach constantly. She is safe here. I see her get up only to go to AA meetings. It has been a beautiful thing to see, after all her troubles, the women in the program here have surrounded her. They call all throughout the day to check on her and a different woman picks her up every night to take her to a meeting. I have dropped her off at meetings quite a few times and she can always find a ride home. The women sometimes come in and talk to me. She has what's called a sponsor and a homegroup and spends every moment that she's awake in recovery. It is as if she is recovering from a physical illness. I always said that she is worth helping, she looked a bit crazy and acted even worse, but she was worth it, I always knew it wasn't her, it was the drugs and the alcohol talking. I had to convince the doctors in the various hospitals and institutions she landed in during these last 2 years that she was worth helping. If they only knew her they would know how special she is, and that it isn't her they are talking to right now, it is the drugs. The first good night of sleep any of us had in years was the day her father dropped her off at Bowling Green.

Now she is starting to look for jobs, though I don't know what she is capable of at this stage. All I can do is be here, be supportive, and pray. I worry that she will relapse, disappear again, but I also believe she has found the help she needs and it is finally working. Time will tell.

Ellen, Age 69

Baltimore, Maryland, 2022

I've been retired for over 5 years now and have come to the decision that it is time to leave Baltimore. I tried to make a life for myself here and as I get older the crime in this city seems to get louder and more unacceptable. I feel as if I am always a mother first, and now I am going to move out to Minnesota to live closer to my three children, Brian, Megan and Nicki, and all of my grandchildren that are there and even one great-grandchild and another on the way. I don't like the sound of being a great-grandmother because I think it makes me sound old, but secretly I have already bought a baby seat for my car because I am so excited to be with the little ones again. I am sad to leave Sarah and Chuck behind, they have stayed in the area they were raised, but I feel it is time to move on from this chapter. In my retirement, I have to watch my finances and in their wisdom, my three kids in Minnesota have chosen a very affordable part of the country to live in, I should be able to get a decent house to grow old in. I have always dreamed of retiring and living on the water, and I've decided that any body of water will do, be it lake, ocean, river or stream. I am sure I will find something and mostly I just pray. I am sad to leave my church here in Baltimore, the first community I have felt a part of in years.

Two years after Marcia sobered up, my sister Sheila passed away unexpectedly. Her loss left a hole within the family that has yet to be filled, and it has hurt every one of us. Sheila remained steadfast through the years, she was always good and she never changed. Behind the scenes she was helping all of our family, always reliable and willing to give what she had. Before she died, our youngest sister Sharon came into town from Vermont and the three of us spent days together catching up. We talked about our mother, Gladys, our children and our lives through the years. I look back on that as a gift, that we were able to have that time together. As for Sharon, against all odds, she lives a life without resentment and has worked through the pain of what she lived through. She is kind and loving, and wise, married with children of her own.

My Stepmother has become the matriarch of this family tree, and after the loss of my father in 1989 she remained a part of our lives. The family relationship with her developed into one of respect, reliance and strength. She is our rock and stability, and brings us all together.

My children have gone through moves, marriages and divorces in their lives, they've all got children or pets in Marcia's case, of their own. Megan has become a very unique and loving mother to her two children and has enough character and personality to outshine us all. Through the years her life has been intertwined with Nicki's, her identical twin. The night Nicki was in the accident, Megan had been calling her for hours, knowing something was wrong. In 2017 our family got the call that Nicki had been in a car accident and her life was on the line. I dropped everything, and it was a lot at the time because Chuck had just had his first child and I was helping care for the baby. But, with Nicki on the edge of death, I knew I had to go to her. I flew to Minnesota to find her unconscious in a hospital bed, hooked up to machines with tubes everywhere. Her arm was gone and I noticed her legs were crushed and looked to be turning black – she was rushed back into surgery and the doctors saved her legs with only minutes to spare. She has lost most of the muscle in her legs and walks with a cane now, but it was a victory the first time she was able to speak. No-one wanted to tell her she lost her arm in the accident, and we found out that she remembered being crushed and trapped for hours in her car that rainy night. Nicki was found in a ditch in the woods on a desolate route by the grace of God, when a policeman noticed skid marks on the road early in the morning and pulled over to hear her screams. All of that is behind us now, but the scars of the accident have left their mark on her body and her spirit. She will always be disabled now, but in her triumph she has become a resourceful, respectable young woman and was the fourth of my six children to become a home owner. She lives by herself in Minnesota, Megan is minutes away and her daughter and granddaughter visit all the time. I am proud of my twins,

43

I enjoy watching who they are as adults, as parents, as sisters and friends.

Brian left Alaska after 20 years and now lives with his children in Minnesota, close to Megan and Nicki. It is a relief to have him back with everyone and his return changed the family dynamic, bringing us all back together in a way. He is a very good father, raising his two boys on his own and now supporting his step daughter as well. Having Brian around has been one of the finest moments for us.

When my oldest daughter turned 50, we took a girls trip to the beach and enjoyed celebrating with her, as Marcia had turned 40 that same year. These are big milestones and I enjoy the way we pick up right where we left off, whenever any of the kids gets together. Sarah has been a nurse some 30 years now, and she is good at it. I have always known how special she is and at her work she shines for those qualities. Since she stayed in Pennsylvania, it was she who recognized when her father needed to go to the doctor and she kept an eye on him through the years, he was a bit stubborn and she is one of the few women he'd listen to about his health.

Chuck stepped in and took care of his father at the end, the last year that Steve was alive. It was a shame to see how he deteriorated so quickly, but after Steve's second wife was paralyzed in a car accident he started to unravel. He moved to Florida when she passed away, a place he always wanted to be, and when it was time he came back to Maryland and lived with Chuck until he entered the nursing home. Chuck's little girl was the apple of Steve's eye! I don't need to tell any more of Steve's story, but I can say that at his end, I was probably his closest friend and we spoke on the phone a few times a week before he passed away in his sleep last summer.

I can almost leave Marcia out of this story now because I believe she is finally okay. When you look in her eyes you can see she has at last forgiven herself. She did suffer a relapse in 2014 and it took me by surprise, but I went to her 1 year anniversary when she started over and I think that by the Grace of God, she may turn out alright. She is married now and lives in Denver with her husband who is also in recovery. They just packed this entire house, all 4 apartments and my storage unit into a U-Haul and drove it across the country for me. I am going to follow soon. She has turned into the one in our family who deals with challenges for us, she is the one I call when I need something addressed. She has a way with people and can solve some of the most complicated issues. It was she who made the arrangements for Steve when he passed away last year. She has stepped into life with grace and purpose, and now I believe she has found redemption.

Ellen, Age 70

Minnesota, 2023

I've been staying with my daughter Megan in the house she rents from Marcia, here in Springfield and have finally settled on a house to buy of my own. This year is starting out with some complicated and sad family news. In February the family gathered around my stepmother's death bed as she passed away, my eldest children stayed by her side when she was brought to the hospital and she passed that very same day. I have been responsible for her estate and all of my nieces, nephews and brother in law have come together with love and generosity to see that her wishes are acknowledged. It is apparent that her role in our family really was that of a kind and loving matriarch. It has been sad to lose her and knowing what a devoted Catholic she was, it is comforting to know she has found her place in Heaven and can be with her loved ones again.

I was shocked and devastated to find out that my sister Judith who I had become close with in our adult years, passed away on the same day. She died at home and as unfortunate as it is to admit, she seemed to have inherited our father's love of alcohol, as well. She was found in her bed with her adoption paperwork and that same birth certificate that my Mother died trying to retrieve, I had given it to her when we met. She passed away the week before the 52nd anniversary of our mother's murder. I know that Judith loved the Lord. She was the pianist at her church and I believe with all my heart that she is in Heaven now with our Mother, and that God knew her heart. When I went to her funeral, I attended a Sunday service at her church and my daughter Marcia sat at the silent piano and played for the church service.

Now that I am here in Minnesota, it has become clear to me that God did have more work for me to do. My youngest, Nicki, has just been diagnosed with cancer and is about to start radiation and chemo treatments. She will stay with me while she goes through treatment and I will be able to care for her and take her to her appointments and all I can do is pray that God is not ready to take her too.

III

Part Three: Marcia

Marcia's story begins in childhood, raised in a religious Northeastern household, quite sheltered from the world, along with her 5 siblings and both parents. As a child she is curious, talented, funny, outgoing and trusting, this naivete she would not recognize until it was almost too late. Her story is one of second chances, tragedy, life on life's terms and self forgiveness, forging a path through this world when she felt she was not meant to survive.

Marcia

Pennsylvania, 1989

Even though it was a long time ago I remember when we moved here to Pennsylvania, because I really liked the kids in my neighborhood in Delaware. Mommy says we outgrew that house and now my Aunt Shelia lives there, so I can go back whenever I want. We play in the cornfields and the woods here and when it's time to come home for dinner someone rings the bell out back and we all go back to the house. My parents put in a giant bell on the deck by the pool and said that if there is ever any trouble we are supposed to ring the bell and someone would come, and whenever we hear the bell if we aren't home we need to get there. It is a good system that we all understand, and it's good because most of the neighbors are Amish and we can't play with them so we have to travel for miles to find any kids out here. I can only remember one time I got into trouble in the pool. My older brother's football friends were playing 'smear the queer' and I was the queer, that's the person holding the football, and everybody tries to get the ball.

Some jerk held me under water until I couldn't breathe or fight anymore and took the ball from me and I started screaming and crying and I ran in and told my Daddy and he came out and scared the living crap out of that guy. He left, I got the football back, and ruined their game. I usually tell on my brothers and sisters if they're being bad.

There is a pond on the side of the house at the bottom of a big hill. My brothers built a ramp so we can ride our scooters and bikes down the hill, fly over the ramp and into the pond. The only problem with that is our bikes get lost in the mud at the bottom of the pond and we have to dive around to find them, we are all good swimmers. Brian got us some rope and now we tie our bikes to our ankles, and we don't lose them. When we're not in the pool or the pond we have adventures in the woods and can go for miles exploring. Sometimes we play in the barn or the grain silo, there's all kinds of stuff to get into. Since I'm in the middle, I play with Brian who's also in the middle. The twins have each other and so do Sarah and Chuckie, each one of us has a built-in friend. I always get stuck playing GI Joe but Brian never wants to play with my cabbage patch dolls! Half the time I guess I'm with the twins and Brian is with Chuckie, it just depends on what we're up to. Daddy is usually out in the fields on his machines, pushing dirt around. We take our trash out to the barn and burn it, and that's how he keeps busy. Sometimes he gives us rides around the field in the mouth of the backhoe, it's like having our very own roller coaster. Sometimes he takes us to work with him and we get to build houses just like we helped build this one.

Marcia, Age 8

Every night we always have dinner together as a family. The kitchen is the size of a restaurant and Daddy built our kitchen table to be big enough for all eight of us. Mom always has a home cooked meal ready for us every night before she goes to work at the hospital. She's a nurse and she delivers babies. We get to go to the hospital and see where she works sometimes, her friends there love us. I'm in music lessons, voice, chorus, ballet, tap and jazz. I tried gymnastics but wasn't very good and I never play any sports. I play the piano by ear and got thrown out of my lessons, two different teachers will not teach me because they play me a song and then I play it back to them, in the key I know. I haven't bothered to try to learn reading notes when I already know how to play it, so they won't teach me. I come home from church or the movies and play whatever songs I hear, and I love playing the piano. Brian plays the trumpet, and he always practices outside on the deck.

And I love iceskating on the pond either here or at Grandmom and Poppop's house. We go over Grandmom and Poppop's every Tuesday and have Elios pizza and brownies. They have the best sledding hill and in the winter time we are always there when it snows so we can go sledding. My cousin Jonathan is fun to go sledding with, and he always gets the best new sleds every year, too. Poppop will check the ice every day until he says it is safe to go ice skating on and all of us go ice skating, my parents, cousins, aunts and uncles and grandparents. The best is when the pond is all ice and you get five people on a toboggan and go down the giant hill and all the way across the pond. We have bonfires and picnics down there all year round. If it isn't ice we go fishing, and can only swim where there's sand because of the snapping turtles. I like to help my Poppop with the horses. We

53

go to the barn and feed them oats and scraps in the mornings, let them out and have to shovel out their stalls, I throw hay down from the loft for him. At night all the horses come back to the barn and we close them in. Poppop doesn't need to mow because they keep all the grass trimmed and it is very important never to let the gate open when we come down the long driveway. My Grandmom brings me to help her collect eggs and feed the chickens, and sometimes we make her special dandelion soup and walk out to the edge of the property to pick dandelions. My grandparents say that they are Pennsylvania Dutch, and they have another language they speak sometimes. Oh, they don't quite get along with the Amish, but they certainly shop at their stores and stands. We pick Amish kids up on the road sometimes and give them a ride to school, usually when the weather is bad. Everyone around here does it, they all go to the same school and learn in one tiny room.

Whenever we are with Grandmom and Poppop they take us to their church events, they are always having cookouts at Nottingham Park and it is one of my favorite things to do. If we aren't at the beach, we spend 4th of July with the whole family and neighboring farms at my grandparents and watch the fireworks. But me, I'd rather be at the beach any day. I could live there! We usually go to our beach house in Delaware every summer and my parents trade off grownups to watch us. The house is usually full of cousins all summer long. I learned how to jump waves and boogie board in the ocean from my cousin Robbie and my big brother Chuckie. Some days we spend the whole day at the water slides in Fenwick, Mom and Aunt Shelia wear their giant sunglasses and coat us all in Coppertone on the hour. They pack sandwiches and pool snacks and we don't leave until it gets dark. Then we sometimes play mini golf or go to the boardwalk. There's a restaurant at the boardwalk in Ocean City where we can eat for $4 each and we have to wait in line for them to open, it's the Paul Revere's Smorgasbord. We can eat whatever we want! My favorite times are 4th of July at the beach, the whole family goes to the boardwalk and camps out on a big spot with blankets and chairs and then at night we lay back and watch the fireworks. We usually go to the rides at the pier a few times a year, I ride with the twins on the smaller rides but now I'm getting tall enough to ride the big ones with Brian and Chuckie. I love summertime.

Marcia, Age 13

Elkton, Maryland 1994

We've been in public schools for two years now. I found out when we moved here that I'm fat and I'm a nerd. I never used to get made fun of in the Mennonite school but here kids are always getting picked on. I sit with the other fat nerds in my class and that's who I hang out with. I'm going into high school next year, Elkton, that's where my brothers go. They are cool, they are both into sports and choir and they have a lot of cool friends. Unfortunately, Chuck and his football friends still play smear the queer and they are a lot bigger than they used to be, and I'm always the queer. I won't play that game in the pool anymore, though we did take the bell and we have that here. At this house we have a big in-ground pool, and my Dad had one too at first. They divorced when we moved here with my Mom.

Sarah got married to Joel when we lived in Pennsylvania. She picks up me and the twins sometimes and we have 'special day' where we go to her house and spend time with her. Joel likes cars and works at the Tastycake factory near where they live in Pennsylvania. Since Mom doesn't buy a lot of food, sometimes he brings home trays of honeybuns for us and it is great. Sarah always feeds us and she is teaching us how to cook, since we don't get to spend as much time with Mom as we used to she has kindof stepped in. She brought me out for Chinese food once and it was the first time I ever had it. She makes little things special, ever since she started driving she knew how to find the good playgrounds and would always take us. I've been to work with her sometimes when she goes on hospice visits, I like the old people she helps and I sing to them. They live in a trailer and have a little boy named Tommy, we get to babysit and he is so cute!

Sometimes my cousin Little Craigie takes us to the roller rink, I have good skates and we shuffle around the rink to the beat. I'm good at roller skating and I've always liked it and since he got a car we get to see him now. I was just thinking about my old dog, Sandy. We have always had one toy poodle and at least two fluffy cats in our household. But when Sandy got ran over and died, my parents never explained what happened to her, though I was there when it happened, it was the only time I've seen my Dad cry. I used to go out to the barn and call her name every day, watching for her to come back leaping through the fields but she never did. Eventually I just gave up, but my parents knew she was dead and didn't ever explain it to me that she wasn't coming back. I know about death now because my Grandad Neat got cancer and died. I liked him, he would take me around his great big garden and show me the vegetables he was growing. He had rows and rows of good tomatoes and cucumbers, and we would sit out there in the sunshine on the farm, crunching on fresh cucumbers. He played guitar and when he died my Grandma gave Brian his guitar, Brian can play and he sings really well. Some of the best moments are when we all sing together, it doesn't happen much but it is a beautiful sound the way our voices harmonize.

I feel responsible for the running of the household when Mom is at work. She works the night shift and sleeps all day, and I like to have dinner ready when she gets up to go to work and we always eat as a family. It is hard to come up with meals from what we have but I get creative. There are always steaks in the freezer and a lot of times Brian will put one on the grill for us. If we are lucky there will be Diet Cokes in the fridge, but that rarely happens. My Mom likes Diet Coke, but mostly we drink tea and water. We know to always brew more tea when we finish the pitcher, and Mom will only use Our Own tea bags. I am in charge of the shower schedule and I know when everyone is allowed to take their turn, and if people get out of line I call my Mom at work. Her coworkers always know what I'm calling about. My Mom will work a lot on holidays so if we can get brought over to the hospital, we will bring her a plate. Now that Chuckie drives he doesn't mind doing it. He will even take us to amusement parks sometimes if we are lucky – we collect the soda cans that have coupons to Six Flags and get discounted tickets from the grocery store. My cousin Robbie always goes with us and they ride the scariest roller coasters, I will only ride one if I have one of them with me to keep me safe.

We had to get rid of the beach house after the divorce and now we go down to the beach whenever Mom's friends will let us stay, or Aunt Shelia takes us whenever she gets a place for the week. Summers get very hot and we have to open all the windows and turn on the attic fan to cool the house down at night, it sounds like an airplane and creates a wind tunnel that slams all the doors and blows the curtains upside down. Thankfully we have a pool and spend pretty much every single day in it. In the summer I don't have to take showers, I just jump in the pool. There is a group of guys that ride go-carts around the neighborhood here and one of them comes over here all the time. We do not have gocarts anymore but we used to ride them around the farm a lot. He's my only friend, and he's not even my friend, he's my brother's. Me and the twins try to keep occupied and we watch a lot of old Shirley Temple movies, I can't count how many times I've seen Heidi. We use the camcorder and make home movies and then watch them. I have a keyboard that makes beats and a karaoke machine with two tape decks and I am always mixing songs and recording music. I like to play the piano when I get sad or upset. In the winter it gets so cold that we all huddle around the fireplace in the living room with all the doors closed, and we have blankets over the curtains on our bedroom windows to keep the cold air out. We aren't allowed to touch the thermostat and we freeze all winter long. Mom tells us to put more clothes on, but it's never cold at Sarah's and sometimes we get to spend the night. We see our Dad once in a while but not on any regular schedule. He always tells us he loves us. He has a new wife now and she's better than any of the women he dated after the divorce. One time we were staying with Dad after we left Pennsylvania and we wanted to go see all our old friends at church. Dad took us one Sunday and when we went in there no one would talk to us and they all acted like they didn't know who we were, I was shattered. I miss my friends from the Mennonite school, and I miss having friends. Sometimes I worry about going to Hell and I get scared if I accidentally hear worldly music, and Chuckie plays it in his car. I know that I will have to burn in Hell forever if I sin so I am always very careful and try to be a good Christian. I am pretty sure those rules all still apply even though we don't go to church as much any more.

I can't understand why my parents divorced, I didn't know there was anything wrong. I've never seen my parents get mad at each other or fight like us kids do. Then again, I never saw them hug or kiss each other, either. Most of what I feel these days is confusion, I don't really understand why everything changed and why we had to lose everything.

Marcia, Age 16

Elkton, Maryland 1997

I found out they were lying about Hell, it took me some time but I figured it out. I can't wait to turn 18 and none of these people will be in charge of me any more. I'm 16 and I look like a grownup. I smoke, I've already had boyfriends, I've tried drugs and drinking, I've been to raves and Phish shows and I even go to bars, I just wash the big M for minor off my hand as soon as I get in and I do what I want. I get stoned and drunk whenever I feel like it and I don't care what my Mom thinks. Drugs aren't even that bad! In fact, they're great! We have parties when she's at work on the weekends, and we go to boarding school all week.

I'm a vegetarian because I am not having an animal die for me to eat it, it's disgusting and barbaric and I can't get the image of that poor deer out of my head. I just play my guitar and sing Grateful Dead songs and listen to folk music. I subscribe to the peace love and happiness concept and am so sure I was born in the wrong decade. Let me rewind this and start with high school. That's when I found out it was all a lie.

First, I watched the movie Clueless the summer before high school so I would know what to expect. It wasn't like that movie at all but I got my hair cut short, discovered makeup and got cute little dresses just like they wore. I went to 9th grade at the public school in Elkton, my brothers were already famous and I was instantly cool on their behalf. For the first time ever, someone said I was hot. I really changed the summer between middle school and high school. Since they were cool we started having parties in the pool garage and they always get a keg and Zima. Brian is in a band and they are extra cool, everybody wants to come over and hear them play and we hide the keg from my Mom before she leaves for work and by the time she gets home in the morning everything is cleaned up and put back. Chuck is graduated now but he was a football star and I mean superstar, people know who he is across all the public schools in the county, so the parties we have get pretty big. I drink as much as I can as soon as I find the alcohol and I can never remember anything the next day. Well, after Mom caught us one too many times she sent us back to the old Mennonite school in Pennsylvania, only it is the high school for Mennonites all over PA and that is why they have a dorm on campus. When me and Brian went back there, none of our old friends were allowed to talk to us anymore. It was like church only worse, they literally turn their heads away.

Mennonites shun people, like specifically on purpose, if they sin. They act like because my parents got a divorce, their sin rubbed off on me and some of it might get onto them if they come near me. So I didn't get any hugs or anything other than prayers from my old classmates. It hurt. We aren't even technically Mennonites so I don't know why they're shunning us, it's so messed up. Anyway, that's how I know it's a scam about God sending people to hell for sinning because it doesn't make any sense! Also, though, I do look much different now and I am using drugs and stuff so they do have a little bit of a point but that's besides the point. To be quite honest I'm not clear on what all drugs are, I don't exactly know where to find them I just say yes if someone has something. And I try to experiment a lot. I need to see what I've been missing out on and I need to see why everyone thinks it is so important not to use them. It's a little bit of a rebellious streak I guess. I will say that there have been a few kids die from heroine already, not Mennonites, people I know from the pool hall and coffee shops in Newark. I go down to Main Street and hang out all the time. I know people there and I play at open mic nights, do poetry slams and hang out while my brother plays pool. He's good at pool, and every once in a while we run into our different cousins down there. Any time I can I'll get dropped off at Main Street. There are always crowds of kids hanging around the Newark shopping center and the different coffee shops so there is always someone for me to hang out with. When I can, I take my sisters Ritalin with me and crush it up and snort it all day, it goes well with coffee and cigarettes. I'll crush and snort any pill really, it doesn't always pay off but as long as there's a chance of getting high, I'll try it.

I go to concerts or raves when I can on the weekends, I have some friends from the public school that I meet up with and we go to Baltimore, Philly or just the beach. If there isn't anything going on, we will drive by the frat houses or skid row or any other areas where the students from University of Delaware party, and if we see people partying we just park the car and go in. I figured out that I can usually just walk in and act like I belong there, and I'll drag my friends in behind me. Once in a while we get kicked out but I've found that for the most part, when people are drinking they don't know what's going on and anybody can show up. I have two best friends, I like to stay over at their house whenever I can and they both always have food in their kitchens. I usually wait till everyone is asleep and then I go in and get something to eat, there is never any food at our house and I am always hungry. Once my friend Lori's Mom caught me digging around in the kitchen at night, I was so embarrassed I tried to hide. Though she is usually very firm and strict, this night she must have realized I was just hungry and she helped me make a sandwich, she always fed me after that, and sent food home with me from their BBQ's or family dinners that I could share with my siblings. We never have anything to pack for our lunches. At the dorm we are on the breakfast and dinner meal plan, but not lunch. We just bring a loaf of bread every week and go through the lunch line and pick up slices of cheese, mayo packets, lettuce, tomatoes and pickles from the free fixins bar, but I've been caught a few times and they don't let me do it all the time. Yeah, being hungry sucks! I have friends in my high school who I sit with at lunch and sometimes they share their food with me. It's not my biggest problem I'm just saying it's been a challenge. Most of my friends though aren't Mennonite, and we pretty much all stick together.

My Dad usually picks us up on Fridays and drops us back off at the dorm on Monday mornings but sometimes Brian gets to use Poppop's old truck. Poppop died recently, broke everyone's heart. Now Grandmom will let us use his truck once in a while. Last year Brian was driving us home to Elkton from school in Lancaster one Friday and it takes about an hour on long winding country roads. There are always deer but you can usually see their eyes at night and have time to slow down. Unfortunately, that time one jumped out in front of us he didn't have time to stop and hit it hard. We stopped the truck and both ran out and looked at the deer as it struggled towards death. We were both crying and had no idea what to do, I got down in the road with it and looked in its eyes and I could physically feel it's terror, willing it to use some of my life to get up but it shook and moved it's legs back and forth rapidly and finally just died, and it's eyes went blank. We cried all the way home. We also got in trouble for the damage on the truck, but I had been changed by the deer. There is a song we sing in rounds in chapel, called 'As The Deer' and it goes 'as the deer panteth for the water so my soul longeth after thee, I love you more than any other so much more than anything.' It is one of my favorites, even though they say I'm a heathen, I do love singing in chapel every morning. The next time I was eating meat all I could see was that deer's eyes, that terror, I could feel sadness all over my body like a vice. I had to put the food down and look at it, and I just saw death. The next time it happened we were getting chicken legs for dinner at school and I swear I could see the bird suffering in panic being killed, it's whole death experience grew out of my hand in the food I was holding and I couldn't eat it. That has happened ever since. I see dying pigs and cows, not bacon cheeseburgers or scrapple. I cannot unsee it and that is why I went vegetarian.

I have been trying to explain it to my family so they will all stop eating meat but so far it has only worked on the twins. They pretty much do everything I tell them to. They come out to our garage parties sometimes. It is the end of my 10th grade year in Lancaster, I'm in detention for the whole week and I have been asked not to come back next year. Brian is graduating, he works at the Bible outlet and stopped partying as much.

I took biology this year and every 10th grader gets a frog at the end of the semester to kill and dissect, it's disgusting and I won't do it. When we first met our frogs they were alive, I played with mine and named it. After school that day I had my friend scope out the hallways and spy on the science teacher, she was just about to drop the frogs in boiling water in the science lab and kill them all. They were in boxes of sawdust in the fridge so they would be too cold to move. I used the payphone outside and called the school office and asked for the teacher, and when my friend gave me the signal that she was gone, we ran in and dumped frogs into a pillow case but there were so many of them we ended up just grabbing the rest of the boxes and running out the side door towards the mill stream. I ran with all the frogs to a beautiful sunny area and my friend stayed behind to scout. I dumped them out in the grass and watched as they started to warm up and move and hop away. I took the time to name every one of them, then I threw all the boxes and my pillow case in the millstream and went back to the dorm. I don't know how they figured out it was me, probably because I said I would let them go, but I didn't think anyone was listening. Anyway, I admitted it when I was questioned. I am supposed to pay for the frogs and they are apparently worth $4 each, so that's a $200 fine. I'll never come up with that kind of money but I've heard someone started a fundraiser and parents keep calling in to donate to the frog fund. See? I'm not the only one who thought it was wrong!

Marcia, Age 22

Baltimore Pre Release Center for Women, 2003

Everything happens for a reason, they told me. This too shall pass and God only gives us what we can handle. I am paying for a crime I didn't deserve to survive, I am in the hole again, in the women's prison in Baltimore city. I've been in the hole since Christmas Eve and I think it's almost New Year's Day but I really have no idea, it is dark and I barely see any people down here. An exceptionally nasty guard came through doing a shake down and tossed my bedding out into the hall and ripped all my things out of my locker in the cell I share with 3 other women. She threw all my stuff out and scattered it everywhere. I have a guitar and it's probably destroyed. She said I had contraband and I'm going back to prison to serve my full 10 years. The warden in this facility is decent, she gave me some art supplies to work on my design for the Christmas play backdrop and we already had the play. It was the worst rendition of a Christmas Carol the world has ever known, half of these women can't even read. This guard says those art supplies aren't on my log of belongings and that I'm in trouble for sneaking in contraband. They pulled me out in handcuffs in front of everyone and took me to the holding cell toilet. The guards yelled and screamed that I was using drugs and forced me to pee in a cup standing up and I'm too shy and I can't pee in front of people especially when they are shouting at me. They yell every time they take me for a random drug test like it's a game to them. They laugh and say I'm going back to the penitentiary. They threaten to give me more charges for drugs and say I'm hiding contraband. How the hell would I have drugs in my system, I'm incarcerated!! There aren't drugs here we can't even smoke cigarettes.

This place is insane and I have never encountered anyone like these people who work in this system or any of the inmates, I don't know how to communicate or protect myself and I'm terrified all the time. They come after me and take my stuff and then I get into trouble for sharing. The women I have been in a cell with throughout this experience have all been hardened criminals. They threaten to hurt me, they took my mailing list and wrote to my family friends asking for money, they steal my stamps and paper. It took months for me to figure out how to buy commissary and when I get my order I'm robbed before I even get it back to my cell. I am still a vegetarian and they have special needs diets but the inmates prepare all our food and going to the mess hall is like walking through hell. All the women make out with each other and some of them look and dress like men. I never know where to sit and I'm scared of everybody. Not that it occurred to me why before Grandmom pointed it out, but it appears I am only one of 7 white people in this whole facility and I think they hate me for just being white, but I don't understand why. There were hundreds of women on the grounds of the penitentiary, might even be thousands, when I was in Jessup, Maryland at the MD Correctional Facility for Women and it is maximum security. Inmates all wear a badge and if you have stripes on your badge you're a 'lifer' and max or double max security level. I am considered pre-release status even though I have 10 years, and we are not supposed to be put together on cell blocks but every one of my cellmates has been double-max. They think it's funny to tell me horror stories of young girls like me in prison getting raped with hot curling irons and broken bottles. I didn't even tell anyone why I'm here but they all seem to know, I guess they watch the news in here. I never say a word if I can help it, and there is nowhere I can turn for help.

When my family comes to visit they are searched at the entrance, and it doesn't sound like anyone is very nice to them. I have to get special permission to hug my visitors but I always get a really good hug from my Dad, he comes the most and brings my siblings, friends and grandmom. After a visit the guards say my name over the radio and this one nasty fat black bitch always shows up to strip search me. She comments about my body the whole time while I take my clothes off and makes me strut all over the room it's disgusting. She offers to bring me things here but I don't know what she wants from me. Makes me want to vomit. I met with the chaplain here a few times and she has lent me her guitar. The fact that the chaplain thought I was cool enough to loan me her instrument gave me like 2 cool points within the population and people weren't as horrible to me after that. I should say, I was only terrorized 90% of the time after that. When I made parole they really turned up the heat. It is like a game around here when someone gets parole all the rest of the people try to antagonize them or set them up so they lose their chance at freedom. Freedom has always been so important to me and now look at what I've become. I have the WORD freedom tattooed on my hip in Japanese! That's how important it was to me to not get myself into a situation like this but here I sit.

Once my cellmate read my letter I had sealed ready to mail out and when we were locked in for the night she started terrorizing me. It was sick, she read where I was calling her stupid because she is learning to read and studying books I read in third grade. She is missing most of her teeth, she's short, black and old, and her hair sticks out in a spiral that she wraps with a bandanna and Vaseline and she turns her stupid little tv up as loud as it gets watching Law & Order, go figure. She eats rank tunafish that she mixes in our cell and it stinks the whole place up. She insists on cleaning the floor with free maxi pads and water from the toilet and the free soap they give us and she makes me take my shoes off at the 'door.' She apparently has a friend she was yelling out the window to about how much she hates drunk drivers and killers and that she knows people who have died from drunk driving and she thinks they should all be hung. She went on about it all night and kept telling in detail all the scary stuff she knows that happens to drunk driving killers. The next morning I ran down to the end of the cell block, I was on the upper tier and I hid in the shower until the guard came around doing their morning check. I grabbed the guard and said I was scared of my cellmate and I thought she was going to hurt me and she fucking laughed.

She cuffed me, took me out in front of everyone and said loudly to all the other guards that I was afraid of my cellmate and she was taking me to the warden. That guard totally blew my cover and made fun of me in front of everyone, people I was already on thin ice with. I was supposed to be going to the kitchen where I was a clerk and it was my job, for $1.05/day to type and print menus and labels for the inmate meals. So, instead I was brought to the warden and left sitting for hours in a dark hall, cuffed to a chair. When I was finally brought into a room, there was my smiling cellmate, saying we were friends and she doesn't know why I would ever be afraid of her and they gave me a choice to go on lockdown or back to my cell. I chose lockdown, where I stayed for the next 6 months.

Every time I needed to leave the cell on that block I was hand-cuffed at my wrists and ankles with a chain around my waste and a chain connecting my feet to my wrists and my waste. There was a toilet and sink in my cell but the shower was at the end of the wing and the recreation area was a cage at the bottom of the steps where the payphone was. So I had to get dragged through a gauntlet of women banging their fists, shouting and throwing shit and piss out the food tray holes in their cell doors. The guards all seemed to think it was funny when I fell and they would pull me off balance. Eventually I told people to stop visiting, I never wanted to go use the phone or shower. I did not tell any of my family what it was like and they still do not know, I do not think they can bare finding out how wretched it is. I stayed in the cell by myself talking to myself and coloring friends on the walls. I read the whole Bible and my Mom had the Wilmington News Journal delivered which I would get on Sundays. My Grandma Felicia writes all the time and sends me Catholic prayer cards. She says it is my cross to bare and I get encouragement from her letters. I know I deserve this punishment, I took someone's life and there is nothing I can ever do to make it right unless I take my own life as well. I hate myself for it. I have gone back and forth on the thought of committing suicide, I know my family would have a hard time dealing with that on top of everything else so I've told myself I will just try to get by and I can do it later. If I can make it 10 years, I can do it then.

I do not remember anything about the accident. I usually go into a blackout when I drink. I was living in California at the time and only came home to visit. After I graduated from the Mennonite school I moved down to the beach in Ocean City, Maryland. They had taken me back for my senior year and I did very well and got straight A's. I never completely subscribed to the Mennonite way of life but I did shape up and stop being so terrible to my Mother. I had fun that year and really tried to make the most of it because I did understand they were helping me. I paid attention in class and really applied myself. Testing was always easy for me, I can ace most of my classes without having to study, unless you count math, I just cheat when it comes to that subject. I enjoyed dying my hair funky colors and I did get a few piercings on my face. I kept experimenting with drugs and alcohol all through high school but at least I did graduate and I know my parents were thankful and possibly proud. The summer after graduation my Dad took me to get my driver's license and got me an old Volvo, an awesome vintage car that totally matched my personality. My Mom wouldn't take me to get my license because she always said 'I didn't fight this hard to keep my kids alive only to lose one of them to the road.' How ironic that this happened. Anyway I lived at the beach for two summers and attended community college in between. I worked at the amusement park where anybody could get a job and I ran the bumper boats. I ran into trouble a few times because of my behavior and I did a lot of things in blackouts that I'm not proud of. I started to suspect that drugs were getting in the way of my accomplishments and actually when I went to California I went to a halfway house and started going to NA meetings. I can't say any of it sunk in and I realized that I could still drink I just had to leave the drugs alone, so that is what I did. However, the drinking and blacking out was still happening and I just kindof ignored it, I mean, I was not old enough to drink at the time so I couldn't really have an alcohol problem. It didn't occur to me once that some of my problems could have been related to the way I was drinking. I was really soul searching at the time. I did not know what I wanted to do with my life. I knew that community college was free for California residents and I really wanted a fresh start. Frankly, I had really embarrassed myself in Ocean City one too many times and I needed to move and find out who I really was. I thought it was the East Coast that was holding me back. I only made it six months in California before the accident, I turned 20 there.

I came home to see family on Memorial Day Weekend in 2001, and I was supposed to be in my older brother's wedding. My other brother came home from Alaska, too and we all were supposed to go to the twins graduation from the Mennonite school. When my Dad picked me up from the airport and we went back to his house I was really excited to see my friends from the beach and decided to drive down there. He told me not to go and I blew it off. I went to hang out with some of the girls I used to live with and we all snuck in to a bar like we usually did. At some point I decided to leave and go pick up the love of my life, sure he would fall back in love with me when he saw me again, even though we had broken up. When I picked him up from work we went back to his house and I was just going to stay the night in the guest house but after he rejected me and went in to sleep I left and went back to the bars looking for my girlfriends. I never found them but I did find the bouncer we usually snuck in with and I went to one of our favorite spots and slipped through the door on his arm. I lost him once I got in and started drinking. I forgot about looking for my friends and proceeded to get utterly smashed. I almost think I remember leaving the bar or at least being told to leave, but it is very foggy. The next thing I knew I was in a parking lot with a smashed windshield and I was surrounded by sirens and lights and cops. I did not know how I got there or what they wanted with me. The police asked me to come down to the station with them and I went through an entire interview basically in a blackout. Later on during my trial I read through the transcripts of that interrogation and I do not remember any of it. I certainly never knew until I saw Law & Order playing on my cellmates tv that I had a right to an attorney and a phone call. I don't remember making any calls but my Mom says I called her and told her. In fact, the entire trial is a blur. I was taking antidepressants, I thought I had a problem and was looking for solutions from a psychiatrist and now the problems are much, much worse. If I wasn't depressed at that time I definitely am now. They wouldn't give me my meds in jail where I was taken and I remember falling asleep on a bench in a cell and waking up every couple of hours to guards banging on the doors yelling 'wake up killer! WAKE UP!" Here I was searching for myself, at a stage in my life where I was trying to find out what I wanted to do with my life, who I wanted to be and all I knew up until that moment was that I was a vegetarian, I was artsy, musically inclined and generally a nice person. Then I found out I was really just a monster and a killer. I started to unravel. I didn't understand why the cops were calling me a killer then I was called in to see somebody important in a suit and they told me I drove down the bus lane drunk and I hit a pedestrian and then I

drove away and they found me. The person I hit was going on
& off of life support and he died within a couple of days. I was
transferred to the Wicomico County jail and there started this
journey of facing what I'd done.

I am waiting for my Mom to move into Baltimore city. She is
not a city person and is having a hard time figuring out all of
the requirements for my housing situation so I can leave. I am
allowed to finish my sentence on work release from home as
long as I have somewhere to go within city limits, that's why
I am in this pre-release center. I hope the warden will get me
out of the hole when she gets back from Christmas break and
I'm not sure what is taking so long but I'm pretty scared. It's
probably God again, needing to get my attention and help me
reflect on this last few years.

Marcia, Age 27

Bethesda, Maryland 2008

After I got off home detention I transferred my parole to the
furthest part of the state I could get, so I moved to Bethesda
on the edge of Washington DC. I went to college and had to get
permission documents from my parole officer to leave the state
and every time I went home to see my family in Delaware or
Pennsylvania I had to be tracked. It was hard for me to find a
job on home detention but I was required to be working. I had a
phone book and I called all the coffee shops down the list asking
if anyone was hiring. No-one wanted to go through the trouble
of faxing my home detention officer a statement so I could come
out and fill out an application and my second time through the

same list, one guy finally agreed. We did my application over the phone and he helped me get approval to come in for an interview. It was my only shot at getting a job and the place was called The Daily Perk. When I got to the address the coffee shop was located inside the Federal Court House!! The place was crawling with cops and lawyers and security and the sight of handcuffs made me want to barf but somehow it worked out. Dwaine helped me find some semblance of self respect again, and he very carefully guarded my secret. He taught me all about big band and swing music and we drank the world's best coffee. He was legally blind and that's why his coffee shop was in the courthouse, but he could kind of see out of one eye if he stood the right way and leaned in. I became friends with the lawyers, cops and US Marshalls, and no-one ever knew I was a criminal. We used to get a real kick out of it, the irony of that situation. I laughed with Dwaine, he was funny and made me feel better about myself. During that time period I also was court ordered to go to AA meetings but I honestly don't recall much about any of it. My landlord was a sober member of AA, another very ironic part of the story, and he would come by and take me to meetings sometimes. We became lifelong friends actually and would play music together. He is one of the few people who know what I've done, I've never told a soul. He would stop by and then act surprised when I answered the door and go 'Oh I was hoping you'd be home!' just to make me laugh. I gradually came out of the dark abyss of self-destruction and self hatred. I started to feel human again. I got off the antidepressants eventually and got some therapy. I used to see a minister for counseling at a church on the street where we lived in Baltimore. She would communicate with the Parole & Probation office on timing so I could get out of the house and walk down to see her, and she gave me the first notion of forgiving myself. She suggested I try it and I would say sure but deep down knew I was still holding onto suicide as an option. I played the organ and piano and sang and played the guitar a few times at that congregation, I hope she knows how much she helped me. Probably every person in those days was strategically placed into my life at just the right time.

I fell for a cute bankruptcy lawyer from the courthouse and when I moved to Bethesda we dated for a while. I eventually left him, I think I was too scarred to be in a relationship and I got my own little basement apartment. I started hanging out with a retired pro football player and he is the one who helped me get into modeling, and I had a lot of exposure to pro athletes in those days. I was slim and pretty and did hair and fashion runway modeling for all different salons and artists around DC. We didn't last long but remained on good terms. I went to Art School and aced every class though I never studied. I had friends in college and never told any of them my secret, no-one knew why I didn't drive but it took years for Motor Vehicle to give me my driver's license back and when they did I had to have a breathalyzer device in the car. I was no longer court-ordered to go to meetings and I did not consider my accident to be in any way related to alcoholism, so I stopped going as soon as I could. It was easier to bury the secret the less people knew about it. I am always afraid someone might find out. I worked in a few different restaurants and print shops through school then when I graduated I got a great job at a design studio in downtown DC as a graphic designer. They hired me right at my portfolio show in the National Building Museum. After I left that job I got an even better one at an international nonprofit and I am on the marketing communications team as a graphic designer.

I think I started drinking again as soon as I got off parole in 2006. I remember blacking out through an entire Dave Matthews Band concert and I was pretty upset that I missed the whole thing, lying face down in the mud. I am engaged and live with my fiancé in Bethesda. We have a nice condo and he has money. Somewhere along the way I learned to use my looks to get by and I realized that if I don't look or act like a criminal, no-one would know I am one. I started wearing pearl earrings and a pearl necklace because I think they look innocent. I try to keep my tattoos covered and I don't want anyone to have even a hint of something to suspect. We've been to Greece three times now and I am learning the Greek language from my fiancé and his family. They are pretty upscale and tight-knit and I have to really fake it to act like I belong. His friends all have money and travel the world. Living here has exposed me to the finer things in life and sometimes I just like to show it off. I want my family to see how good I am doing now. I have a brand new car that he bought me right off the lot. I really look like nothing's wrong, and that is the only way I am able to live with myself, is just that I look like I'm fine, so I'm fine. We have a fluffy calico cat and a nice condo on the edge of DC, there is a pool in the neighborhood and a gym at the clubhouse. I only have to spend my own money on my student loans and he buys everything else. I've got a designer handbag and designer clothes. When we go out we drink top shelf liquor or expensive wines. Sometimes we go to the nightclubs in DC and the bar tab will be over $300 for just the two of us, we have a good time out but for the most part he is pretty straight laced. I think I may have embarrassed him once or twice from blacking out but it hasn't been a big problem. Once I woke up and all our dishes were smashed all over the floor because we got hammered and started breaking them all for fun. His mother showed up the next day and I was so hungover I could barely walk straight and I didn't want her to come in and see the mess. I made her wait outside while I did damage control before finally letting her in. Sometimes I wonder if she suspects I am a fake.

When I discovered painkillers I found they killed many types of pain, not just physical but emotional and I try to get them from doctors all the time. I go to different specialists and basically exaggerate or plain make things up in order to get them. That is the one thing that comes between us in our relationship, my fiancé says I'm taking too many pills but I just blow it off and tell him to be nice to me. When we fight I make him apologize with an expensive gift and he doesn't always fall for it but usually it works. We are getting married in Greece and his family pretty much took over planning the wedding.

Marcia, Age 30

Baltimore, Maryland, 2011

Things got pretty bad for me for a while there. In 2009 I lost my job at the nonprofit in DC and then things started to unravel. The organization had to do a massive layoff and I was one of the newest hired so I was one of the first to get cut. A lot of people lost their jobs that year. I started building up a tolerance to the painkillers and had to really work at getting enough to keep myself stable. I think I had a herniated disc or something minor when I first got the painkillers and from day 1 I was hooked. I liked to take the whole bottle in a few days and have fun buzzing out at work. I started going to some pain clinics eventually looking for more but I didn't really have any physical pain so I had to be really convincing to the different doctors so they would give me more. I could usually get muscle relaxers and it was also pretty easy to get Xanax, but the opiates were harder to get a prescription for. I would hate to see my health records because it probably says I have all kinds of crap wrong with me that isn't true. I left my fiancé in a snowstorm in February, had all my stuff packed and hidden when I turned up with the U-Haul. He wouldn't let me take my car but insisted I take the cat. He was heartbroken when I left but he wouldn't get off my back about the pills and I didn't want him interfering anymore. It was the only thing that made me feel better, but he would never understand that and I wasn't about to admit it. Once I lost the job I basically threw everything else away. So there I was with a UHaul full of stuff and my cat, rolling into Baltimore in like 2 feet of snow. My old landlord had a house for sale in the ghetto and said I could stay for a while. I remember when he came to see me for the first time in years and he couldn't believe how skinny I was. I dropped into a seizure on the floor and he looked panicked when I came out of it, he was really worried about what he'd just seen and I couldn't explain why that had started happening. I would get a weird feeling then come to on the floor and always have a strange feeling for a little while after it happened, but I just ignored it. I had bigger problems than whatever that was. I needed to get seriously high! I wasn't stable at that place long and eventually had to find somewhere else to go.

In the couple of years that followed I found myself in lower and

lower social circles. I bounced around between living situations and spent all my time looking for 'more.' More, at the end, was any drug or booze I could get my hands on. As much as I could find and as fast as I could get it. I knew about heroine from my teen years but at this time it seemed to be the natural progression of things for me to go see if I could find a bag or a bundle. I lied to the pharmacy and said I needed diabetic needles for something or other and they sold them to me. I was shooting heroine anytime I could get it. I was always on the hunt for pills. I would take coke, ecstasy, even crack on accident once, just to have some kind of substance in my system. I didn't have a job and I rode out unemployment for a while. I had to really stretch that money and it did not buy me nearly enough drugs. I tried to use my looks to get men to buy me drugs or booze but the quantities I was looking for ended up being more than what any sophisticated guy would support. The only asset I had was my brother's old Honda Accord he gave me, and I would let drug dealers use it to make a run as long as they gave me some of their haul. I had to find ways to come up with money and pulled a few freelance design jobs but I wasn't a very good employee and nobody wanted me around. I couldn't get any work done if I was high, and I couldn't get any work done if I wasn't. I started going to the methadone clinic in Wilmington and I stayed with one of my Mother's friends there when I really crashed and burned. I was always trying to find a gig but I was so disgustingly unemployable that everything blew up in my face and it usually dragged down whoever was trying to help me, too.

One night I had been hanging around the tobacco shop that sold all kinds of fake pills and powders, there is a whole industry of legal-not-really-legal drugs that you can buy in those places. I felt like they owed me a refund or some free products or whatever and I was sitting out there in the parking lot calling the guy who worked there with his Dad, over and over and over. This is what I now refer to as 'the bath salts era.' A particularly gruesome trend, this stuff came in a powder that gets consumed by smoking or drinking or snorting it. It didn't really matter how it got consumed, the effect took place quickly and lasted for weeks. It was like being on LSD, PCP, weed, crack-cocaine and booze all at once. It felt horrendous, and the only thing I wanted to do when I was on the stuff was more of it. I would go into blackouts or perhaps brownouts, for weeks at a time and resurface wherever the hell I turned up when it wore off. I would pee myself instead of going to the bathroom, and I never ate anything but ice cream and usually left it out all night to melt. I had messy hair full of chocolate syrup, I was usually wearing heels and ripped jeans with a little tank top but I almost always lost or ditched my shoes and I went barefoot most of the time. The night I was hanging out at the bath salts shop I must have started having seizures. I know I was acting really weird and scary, wandering around the parking lot like a maniac. They called an ambulance which took me to a hospital in Wilmington. I don't know how long I sat in there but they never admitted me, they told me I was obviously intoxicated and they were just going to let me sit there till it wore off, so I left. Now I'm barefoot I think, walking through the small city of Wilmington, Delaware and I start going into bars trying to *get me something to drink.* I had come up with a conspiracy theory, too. Someone was after me or owed me something or who knows what. I didn't have my purse or any money, phone or ID because I was always leaving it places. I determined the best thing to do was call the cops.

I went into a bar and asked for a drink and asked them to call the cops for me. Really, they were going to call the cops ON me anyway. When they got there I asked for them to take me down to the station because somebody was after me but I couldn't quite put together the whole scenario on who was after me or why and I was slurring and stumbling and probably looked like I escaped from the mental hospital. I couldn't remember where I lived so they couldn't take me home. I had no idea where my car went, so they couldn't or wouldn't take me back there. All I could remember was my old phone number in Delaware where my Aunt Shelia and Uncle Randy lived, so they called them and my uncle, the cop, came and picked me up. He just so happened to know that I lived with my brother Chuck and got me there safely. It is one of the more embarrassing moments because I was probably covered in piss, too.

My brother tried everything to get me under control. He had to forbid me from smoking in the house because I kept passing out with a cigarette burning in my hand. He worked the night shift and I would spend all night long getting high on whatever I had, drinking heavily and looking through the blinds. I always thought someone was coming to get me and I thought he was always about to get robbed or busted or something fictional. He and his wife let me stay there with my cat, I had a small bedroom upstairs. I can't count how many times I came to passed out across the litter box. I kept my cat in my room and her litter box took up some of the floor space, and I was always falling into it. I found my way to his place of employment a few times, inebriated and always with a different man, and I would find some reason to need something and always caused a scene. Once I went to a place he didn't even work at anymore and just embarrassed his best friend, instead. I don't remember all the institutions I went to during the bath salts phase but I know there were at least two mental hospitals. In one I vaguely remember being in a padded room tied down to the bed because they probably thought I was dangerous. My family was always tracking me down, trying to keep me from hurting myself or someone else. What was really going on was that I was suicidal because I hated myself for killing someone and I had no way to get through it other than trying to numb the pain with drugs and alcohol. I couldn't NOT drink, I absolutely had to drink to survive. Sometimes if all I had was booze, just a couple of drinks got me completely wasted and blacked out drunk, but then other times I could go through an entire box of wine and not feel intoxicated in the least. I can recall a few comments here and there about my drinking, or about me drinking and driving, or about me driving but I couldn't hear the pain in their voice or comprehend the fear in their eyes, so great was my own pain and fear.

The last Christmas before I got sober I was supposed to go spend the night with my Mom at her house in Baltimore. I really, really needed to get high. It was Christmas eve and my connection kept blowing me off but I drove all the way out to near where the guy lived in Delaware and waited in my car for hours as the snow got deeper, calling him over and over to come and meet me and give me some stuff. He never did and after midnight I finally gave up and drove to Baltimore, I was sick as a dog and I needed drugs. I think I just drank down my Mom's limoncello or some liquor she had from a cooking class but I managed to get through it. There was nothing worse than being drug sick. Nothing, it is like your skin is on fire and your stomach is inside out. In those days the nightmares happened every time I fell asleep, that is one of the reasons I tried to stay up all the time. As soon as I fell asleep and started dreaming, I was all of a sudden a serial killer. I was axe murdering people, shooting people, running people over, I've had every single demonic scenario I could dream up of what might have happened in my accident. It was torture to sleep and I woke up screaming and crying, sweating all over and shaking.

I started seeing my Dad hanging around Chuck's house when he was in bed or at work, or my Mom would turn up and take a shift, then my sister Sarah would come by. They were babysitting me, I didn't realize it at the time but they knew my life was on the line. One particular bout, I don't quite recall what led up to it, but I happened to be in the car with my Mom and during the conversation she offered the idea that I might try out going to rehab. I knew the place she was talking about, because Chuck had told me all about it. Some place in Pennsylvania where they had a pool and a spa and good food like a spiritual retreat or a vacation getaway, he made it sound real nice. By the end of the car ride it was my idea that I wanted to go there. As soon as my Mom had my agreement, she put the plan into action. Before I knew it I was getting into my Dad's car and he was driving me to Bowling Green in Toughkenamon, Pennsylvania. That's not far from his house and he stopped to let me get a sub on the way and he let me know that I was probably not going to feel much like eating in the next few days and I should try to eat what I could then. My brother turned up the next day with a bag packed for me and that is where I got help.

There was no pool at Bowling Green. No spa or massage therapy or anything fun or fancy, it was almost like a camp for poor grownups out on some farm surrounded by fields and a sludgy green pond. All the meetings and classes were held in the barn. Yeah, a real barn. I was sick as hell and detoxed for a solid week. They let me smoke but wouldn't give me any pills. Every time the nurses opened the medication window I was first in line, begging for them to give me anything to make me feel better. They withheld all the good stuff, and assured me that they had checked my vitals and I'd seen a doctor and they all confirmed I wasn't dying. They encouraged me to hang in there and just ride it out, and assured me it wouldn't kill me. My hair was a big fat knotted mess, dreadlocks of every length and it hadn't been brushed since my sister did it for me a few months earlier in the mental hospital visitor's room. One of my roommates in the detox ward who happened to be a very large black woman, combed it out for me and it took her nearly 3 hours. She was very kind about it and I know it was revolting. I was willing to admit that I had a drug problem, I mean it was pretty obvious. But I did not identify as an alcoholic until they almost let me out on Memorial Day Weekend. My government insurance ran out and it had only been a week or two, and I was counseling myself on how I would get through Memorial Day weekend out there in the world without drinking OR using drugs. I determined that, even though I normally had standards and did not drink for Memorial Day weekend in honor of the accident, I was going to have to anyway. I knew I needed to stop drugs but I couldn't just be sober, I would never survive it. It's strange how I could be suicidal and self-protective at the same time. When the rehab called everyone's names to leave that next morning, no-one called me. I had my bag ready and I was all prepared to drop the bar even lower, and get drunk as soon as I was free. Eventually a counselor brought me into their office and explained that my insurance had come through and approved a few more weeks. I brought my bag back to my room and looked out the window and I swear God came right through the clouds and shone into my heart and told me I was going to be okay. It dawned on me that it was the exact 10 year anniversary of the accident and I had made it this far and I couldn't kill myself because I was in there, and there was God in the window giving me a second chance at life. I realized that I wanted to live. I sincerely and with all my heart wanted to be alive. It hit me like a ton of bricks in the gut, OH MY GOD. I'M AN ALCOHOLIC. All of a sudden all the memories came rushing in and the puzzle pieces started fitting together. Every time I got into trouble I was drinking. Once I started drinking, I never knew what was going to happen and could not stop once I got started, I was powerless over alcohol. The next meeting I went to in the barn I introduced myself as an alcoholic this time and dropped the drug addict title. I realized they were bringing in meetings of Alcoholics Anonymous and I clung to every word. I could hardly remember anything about the program from any of my past exposures but it suddenly all started to sink in. I was having aha moments left and right. It was like the whole world changed colors on me and nothing was ever the same again. When my Dad came to see me he was crying, and he told me he hadn't slept in months until he dropped me off there. He saw the change in my eyes and knew I was finally getting help.

When I got out of rehab the only person left willing to take me in was my Mom, so I circled back to Baltimore yet again. We talked about my aftercare plans and I was convinced that the help I needed could be found in AA. The day I left Bowling Green this grouchy old black man put his hands on my shoulders and looked me dead in the eyes and said "I don't care where you end up, wherever you do, you get to a meeting today and you put up your hand and you ask for help, because you need it." So that's what I did. I ended up on Mom's couch in Baltimore city. We pulled out one of her bicycles and it had a rusty chain so she used the only oil in the house which was a garlic olive oil and greased it up, got me on my way and I rode that garlic bike to a meeting in Canton Square. I was already sick from the drugs and I looked terrible, and now I smelled like garlic too. I sat in the middle of a group of women and as soon as I had the chance I put up my hand and asked for help. Women surrounded me after the meeting and they started a phone list for me and they took down my phone number and one of them asked where I lived and told me to be outside the next night at 7pm and she would pick me up and take me to a meeting. At that second meeting I did the same thing, and the same thing happened. I rode to at least one meeting every day with a different woman. For months the chain kept on going, I never missed a day. I had a hard time getting out of bed and it took everything I had in me to brush my teeth, shower and brush my hair. It felt like my skin was inside out and I was raw from years of pain, guilt, shame and remorse and it was eating me alive. Whenever I was struggling with those things I called down my phone list until someone answered and whoever was on the other line always talked me through it. I got a sponsor and homegroup because those are suggested as a program of recovery. I started reading the Big Book every waking moment and I worked the steps with my sponsor. I will never forget the time I said something about my accident out loud. From the first day in rehab I stopped having the serial killer nightmares. After living on Mom's couch for a few months I had one particularly disturbing nightmare, the same one from the past. I woke up screaming and crying, I couldn't breathe and I was sweating all over, I was in a complete state of panic. I looked up a morning meeting and Mom let me take her car to go. At this meeting there was a speaker sharing for 15–30 minutes then they pick people at random to share and the speaker picked on me first. I was still shaking and sweating and I blurted it all out. That I had killed someone drunk driving and went to prison and just got sober and had a nightmare and it all came spilling out in a jumble of chaos and sad panic. After the meeting people lined up to talk to me and one man waited for everyone and then told me his story. It was almost the same as mine, he had hit and killed a pedestrian driving drunk in Baltimore in the 80's, and he knew how I felt. Here I had held this dark secret for 10 years until I nearly let it kill me, and the first time I said it out loud someone knew how I felt. I was no longer alone. We heard about a man who was celebrating a sober anniversary that coming Friday, and this man had killed his daughter who was in the back seat of his car when he was driving drunk. He said he would pick me up and take me to that anniversary meeting and in the car we decided we would both stand up and announce that we had done the same thing. We did it, and that night, another man came up to me and told me he was driving his motorcycle drunk and his wife went off the back in a wreck and she died, and he was trying to come to terms with that. The connections kept on happening and I met people, one after the other, with my same story. I had a dozen vehicular homicide stories in my pocket by the time I got a job and moved out.

I rented a house with two other women in early sobriety not too far from my Mom's. I had my cat back from my brothers and both of these girls had pets. None of us had much in the way of furniture or belongings but people in AA started giving us stuff.

We all had air mattresses and at night you could always hear someone blowing up their mattress. We came up with enough dishes and donations to stock our household and the neighbors gave us a couch that we hauled in through the front window. I had my stuff in storage for years at that point and finally had somewhere to unpack it. When I went in to get my things out I found drugs in a cookie tin and really beat myself up for missing out on it. I threw the stuff out and I set the flask full of vodka on the stoop out front of our house, it was gone within the hour. I was no longer capable of working as a designer because my brain was pretty fried. I had a hard time talking normally and was always shaking and falling down. Sometimes I would get these electric jolts and fall out of my chair, everyone thought it was funny and they called me 'bath salts Marcia.' I had to come up with nicknames for everyone because I couldn't remember anything. I started working at Starbucks and I never knew if I knew people as customers or AA friends. Once I was walking from our house in Highlandtown and I recognized this lesbian couple and assumed they were going to the same AA meeting I was walking to, so I hopped in their car at a red light. After a few blocks they asked where I was going and I realized that they weren't the AA lesbians, they were the Starbucks lesbians. Thankfully they thought it was funny and took me where I needed to go. Dumb stuff like that is always happening. I don't have a car because I wrecked Chucks before I got sober. I never have any extra money but people in the program still invited me out to eat and would pay for me, and someone would always buy me cigarettes. I was so fried that I couldn't comprehend getting a bank account and my credit was shot, so I had no credit cards either. I had a load of debt that I figured I would never be able to pay off. My roommate let me sign my paychecks over to her and she balanced out a budget for me, took what I needed for rent and utilities and gave me what was leftover to spend. I'm broke, but I have never been happier. My sponsor suggested that I just stick with women my first year and told me not to get in the car with any guys, she suggested I only get phone numbers of women and build a circle of friends from only women. It was a foreign concept and I found that I learned all the neighborhoods in Baltimore and who lived where, so I could know who to ask to go to the different meetings. Probably not having a car is the best thing for me because it forces me to spend time with women in recovery.

There is a big church across the street and I go in twice a week because they let me play the piano in the sanctuary for a few hours. I play out all the pain and sorrow, and it pours out of me onto the keys. The sanctuary is dark and empty when I play and it is the most beautiful sound. Some of the meetings I go to are in a church room with a piano and I like to go early so I can play. An oldtimer in the program says he knows someone who wants to get rid of their piano and is looking into getting it for me. That would be an incredible gift. My roomates and I play music together and have art days and invite tons of people over to our house, we have big parties in AA and someone is always doing something exciting and inviting me.

Marcia, Age 34

Solomon's Island, Maryland, 2015

When Memorial Day came around in 2012 I celebrated my 1 year anniversary of being sober. I had met so many people in AA that the room where my homegroup is was packed wall to wall, no seats left and people standing shoulder to shoulder to hear me. I had a table full of gifts, flowers and cards. I shared my story that day for the first time on a microphone and afterwards my sponsor and a few family members got up and said something. People still talk about my father from that day, he is a big man and he went up to the podium and sobbed into the microphone, thanking those people for giving him his daughter back.

Every year during Memorial Day weekend I always suffered, it was as if the pain and remorse from my accident and time in prison played loudly on a screen through my head until the weekend was over. I started going to therapy again and had to do intense work on my PTSD. I was having panic attacks any time I talked about it or if I ever saw or heard about any car accidents. I was very reactive to people that reminded me of the women in prison, if someone coughed or spoke a certain way, sometimes a switch would flip in my mind and I would go into a full blown panic attack. Sometimes even riding in a car too close to a pedestrian would set me off. I could not sit with anyone behind me and always needed to be near a door in case I needed to escape. I had to slowly walk through the pain of telling my therapist everything that happened in there and it was like torture. Women with long term sobriety handled me through that and would drive me there twice a week and wait in the waiting room because when I came out of a session I could hardly remember how I got there. I learned how to breathe through an attack, I was taught to stamp my feet on the ground and say the date out loud, then I would say out loud where I was at that moment, and what I was doing, and where I was going, how I got there, telling myself facts until it blew over. The panic attacks started to lose their grip on me and eventually completely went away, but it was a very hard road to get there. I had to go on antidepressants during that time, and when the treatment was finished I went back off the medication and am free and clear of it now.

After our lease was up I moved to a different house with another young woman in the program, 2 city blocks up from my Mom's house and could walk back and forth all the time. I was still working at Starbucks then and picked up work catering for someone in the program. I picked up petsitting and any odd jobs I could in those days. I met my boyfriend in the rooms of AA and we started dating and eventually he moved in with me and my AA roommate there. The 3 of us had a blast most days and tons of good parties. We would pile 50 people or more into the house for game night, or have cookouts. I am still a vegetarian after all these years and at first I wouldn't let him bring any meat into the house. He did not have a car when we first met and was taking the bus to work, gym and meetings. He was shy but I introduced him to the crew and he really came out of his shell. My boyfriend isn't from Baltimore but that is where he moved to get sober. The first time I took him over to my Mother's house he asked her if she needed anything done and she gave him a list, and it's been smooth sailing for them ever since. He is like my Dad in some ways because he can build or fix anything. In our early sobriety neither of us were very confident and just plugged away at life. We were always going to events and getting involved in something, whether it was the Baltimore Sobriety Show, a convention or the annual 5k for Recovery, there was always some big event on the horizon to look forward to. We were pretty broke in those days and working starter jobs. Once we had a grocery budget of $20 for the week and went down to the ghetto grocery store and bought what we could to pack his work lunches and for us to get by on, we really stretched our pennies. We both still smoked cigarettes at that time and never really knew where we would get our next pack but started rolling our own to save money. I usually ate at least one meal at work, I would get catering leftovers and any time we were in need we just walked to my Mom's to see what she had.

It was so much fun living near my Mom in recovery, we were always at her house. I think she was blown away at the complete change in my life and was very happy. She knew all of my friends and people would come by just to hang out on her front stoop, she always had coffee on standby. In fact, I got a bag of coffee a week from Starbucks as my single employee perk and I always took the expired stuff before it was thrown out, too. We always had good coffee and working there was the best thing for me. I struggled with memory problems but learning the simple steps of drink recipes and using the register helped me start thinking straight again. Some of the customers there have become lifelong friends. Eventually I found a vehicle I could afford from someone in the program, it was a shitty Ford Explorer that needed a thousand dollars worth of work and she sold it to me for a thousand bucks. I had to borrow the money from my boss at the catering company to buy it and get it on the road and it took me forever to pay her back. My boyfriend, Christian, was the first of us to get a vehicle though, it was an enormous, old rusty gray truck with a cap that you could hear a mile away. It didn't fit into any of the city parking spots. He was very proud of that truck, and my Dad gave him some tools to get started.

In 2014 we got our own place just on the edge of Baltimore, Christian got a job at a large construction site on the waterfront. One of our friends in AA helped him get the job and he was working as a carpenter journeyman on the VA Beach tunnel project where they built the tunnels in Baltimore and then would float them down the Chesapeake to the project in Virginia. That same young man died this year of an overdose and the two of us traveled to Pennsylvania for his funeral. We got a puppy and cherished every moment with her and enjoyed living there. During this time I started checking things off my bucket list that I had always wanted to try and one of them was roller derby. I became slightly obsessed with the idea of getting on one of the Baltimore teams, it is popular there and the sport is pretty brutal. I saved up and ordered myself a really good pair of skates. I happened to live close to the skating rink where the derby girls practiced and I would go there and follow them around, practicing the same moves that they did. That was when I fell and broke my arm, I kept skating that night until it was too swollen to ignore, and drove myself to the hospital. By the time I got there my rings were swollen onto my fingers and the nurses had to work very hard to get them off, I was in a lot of pain from the break and when they offered me painkillers I barely gave it a second thought before saying yes. I called Christian and he came and stayed with me until they sent me home, and I had a bottle of 12 painkillers to go. We decided that he would be in charge of distribution and he held the prescription, even though he was afraid of being exposed to protect his own sobriety, he did it anyway for me. I was speaking at an AA convention that weekend and had been sober for about 3 years by then. We followed the directions and I took the pills as prescribed but they didn't seem to work on the pain. What they did work on though, was awakening that thirst for more, deep dark down inside me. After the convention was over and the pills were gone I went the next week to the orthopedic doctor to get a cast put on. I asked them for pain meds that weren't addictive and got a rather large prescription for Tramadol. They weren't considered a narcotic at the time and I had only used them in the past out of desperation, because they aren't very good. I started taking more than I was supposed to, overdid it a little and one day when my Mom happened to be at our house I was talking to her and dropped into a grand mal seizure. I went to the hospital to get checked out, they said it was the medication and I stopped taking it. When I came home I was in a fog for the next few weeks. That is when Christian was offered a job in Southern Maryland and he got into the carpenter's union. The situation over the seizure and the painkillers blew over, I got the cast off my arm and we moved south. We hit meetings around there but didn't really know anyone except for the people he worked with. My Mom came to help us move and kept in touch with us. I was working at a print shop by then, outside of Baltimore and commuted for a while. Sometimes I would stay at her house overnight and I usually took the puppy with me to work. One day when I didn't have the dog it occurred to me that I could probably go to an urgent care center and tell them I had whiplash and get some painkillers, so I did. Ironically, I happened to run into my sponsor from Baltimore that day before I went in. I had a God-wink right there and it was my opportunity to turn around, and I didn't. I started doctor hopping again and getting painkillers and eventually one night when I was housesitting for someone I decided to drink again. I knew my recovery was shot and I drank hard. Once I had the feeling of opiates in my system the very first time, I could not shake the craving. Looking back on it now, I should have told the doctors in the emergency room that I was a drug addict and an alcoholic and I was allergic to narcotics, but I did not.

I went into the inner city of Baltimore where I thought I could buy some heroine and I couldn't find anyone to sell it to me. I found the drug dealers, but they not-so-nicely told me to get off their corner. I looked up a methadone clinic and started on that again, going every morning. It was complicated to have to get to Baltimore all the time from southern Maryland, and work at the print shop and hide it from my Mom and boyfriend. My tolerance was very high and they would never give me enough methadone to feel good and I started buying the legal-not-so-legal stuff from the tobacco shops again, only by now bath salts are firmly illegal so what they have is something called Kratom, and I took that on top of the methadone and drank. I quickly lost control of the situation. My boyfriend worked the night shift and worked very long hours, we rarely saw each other in our own house. One night I was taking a bubble bath, one of my favorite ways to relax. I had been drinking and he was in the living room watching tv, a night off he wasn't supposed to have. From his perspective, he says he overheard a loud gurgling noise from the living room and turned down the tv to realize it was coming from the bathroom where I was. He barged in and found me in the tub, thrashing and shuddering around under water. He grabbed me by the hair and pulled me up, saving me from drowning. That is when my relapse was exposed, he asked if I had been drinking or something and was blown away when he found out. He was crushed by the betrayal and could not even look at me. He called my Mom and she admitted she was starting to suspect something. The two of them came up with a plan and eventually I landed back in Baltimore, again, at Hopkins Bayview Detox. When we lived in Baltimore, we would take AA meetings to Bayview Detox, along with all the other hospitals and institutions in town, so I knew the place. It was strange to be on the other side and when one of my old homegroup members came in with a meeting, she hugged me and told me they saved my seat.

The road back to recovery was staggeringly difficult, compared to the first time I got sober. Staying sober was no longer easy, and the gift of cravings being removed was denied me by my Higher Power. I had to fight for every sober breath and I wanted to drink more than anything else in the world. I started going back to meetings in Baltimore, living on my Mom's couch again. The same women started picking me up for meetings and I had to start all over. Eventually my boyfriend took me back, but he was very distant and had a hard time letting me back into his life and his heart. He felt like he had been cheated. I was fortunate that he was home the night I almost drowned and was grateful to him, it was hard for me knowing I had lost his respect. I tried once ordering Kratom online and when I took it, it did nothing. The pain was still there, the remorse and shame was even worse. I finally gave up the idea of getting chemical relief from the pain inside of me, and had to work the 12 steps again, I found a new sponsor in Southern Maryland and a new homegroup. I made friends in AA down there and would go to the beach almost every day. This town is on the Chesapeake Bay and there are beaches in all of the neighborhoods. I have always been crazy about sharks and started finding fossilized shark teeth on the beaches there for fun. I would go swimming, take the dog there, lay out in the sun and we had a lot of cookouts there as well. The AAs in southern Maryland had a strong affinity with the bay and many of their parties and get togethers took place there. I met a woman with 30 years sober and she was happy. She would walk and talk with me down the beach. Analyzing my pain and picking through where I went wrong. She was very interested in the Big Book and started reading it with me and a group of women, line for line. I became just as interested in the history of AA as she was.

Around this time I had previously committed to going back to Ocean City, Maryland to speak at someone's anniversary down there. Originally I told the man no, because I knew I would never be able to set foot in that town again and still be able to breathe. The old panic attacks were under control, but going back to that town was another level of stress that I knew I would never be able to overcome. Since the time I had made the commitment I had relapsed. I was about 6 months sober when the date came around. I worked hard with my sponsor, and she helped me get to the 9th step quickly so that I could go to the beach and make my amends with my victim at the scene of the accident. Before I went back to Ocean City I had to find a new conception of God, a higher power that would love and forgive me, so that I might be able to consider forgiving myself. I felt wretched inside, and would go to the beach alone many mornings and watch the sun rise. It was there I found my God, I would walk and pray out loud. I mostly talked to this higher power like a friend, an entity that was beauty and sunlight and waves, and I would look out on the horizon where the sky met the water and picture that as where this power lived. If I needed to know what God looked like, that was it. I had to drop the Mennonite and Presbyterian God I was handed in childhood. I couldn't use my Grandma Felicia's Catholic God either, but I recited her prayers all the time. I knew I held deep and strong beliefs about taking someone's life that I had to overcome and that is why the God of my youth wasn't working. One of my favorite poems is Footprints in the Sand, and if it is real, God carried me many of those days that I walked that beach. There is a God who carried me through prison, and into this life. I knew deep down I had a purpose but not what that purpose was. My gut instinct has always been very strong. I had to face a darkness inside of me that got in the way of my relationships. I worked through victimhood mentality with my sponsor after another particularly ugly disagreement with my boyfriend. He told me I always was the victim but I wasn't always under attack and for once I saw that he was right. My sponsor and I dug back through my past and saw that my coping skills from prison turned me into a poor partner in this world and that I could drop those behaviors. I walked the beach and cried out to God in pain, ashamed of who I had become, and when I hit my knees in the sand I saw rays of light coming out of the water close to me. I went into the water and picked up a crystal that had been reflecting rays of sunshine, and I knew it was a sign. I was forgiven, I felt that. I was going to be ok, I felt that too. I felt seen, heard and protected.

My turning point took place in Ocean City. As I said, I was about 6 months sober at the time. I went to the beach to speak for the man's anniversary and stayed with 4 other women from the program. One of the women had a beach house and we all went down together. They took me to the scene of my accident and the four of them waited in the car while I approached the area. There is a sign there with a plaque on it that says "In Loving Memory Of Alex Alvarez, Victim of DWI, On Behalf of His Family and Friends Please Don't Drink and Drive." I went to the sign and poured out my heart, I don't know how long I was there crying and shouting and talking, I apologized sincerely to him for taking his life, I admitted being angry at him for taking mine, I told him everything and sobbed and sobbed. When I got back in the car no-one said a word, they just drove quietly back to the beach house. During that drive the town came back to life before my eyes. The block of pain and sorrow that coated the good memories from my past started to melt away, and I began to remember the good times I had there as a child with my family. I remembered the boardwalk, the rides, the fireworks, the special moments and happy memories. I felt like I had laid my burden down.

The speaking engagement was smooth and when I returned to Southern Maryland, something had changed in me. I looked in the mirror when I got home and said "I forgive you."

Marcia, Age 37

New Castle, Pennsylvania, 2018

After the experience in Ocean City, things started to change in my life. I took a job as the receptionist at the gas plant project my husband was working on. It was the first job I'd had in a long time with Paid Time Off and health insurance. I started making surprisingly good money and was able to participate in community outreach events for the company. On top of my duties as receptionist, I took on the role of marketing and communications and was responsible for writing the newsletters and creating the electronic news feeds that went out to the workers on the construction site. It was a mega-project, building a LNG plant on the water there in Southern Maryland and there were 7,000 craft and staff employees. I got involved in fundraising and collecting for different drives within the community, on top of going to tons of AA meetings and conventions there. I had established a network of people in recovery and had friends to call on at all times for support. I took my recovery and my life seriously, and knew that if I wanted to survive it was going to take some work. One beautiful sunny day my dear boyfriend took me down to the beach and proposed marriage. Bless his sweet heart he was nervous! He said to me "ok, are we going to do this or what?" I imagine that was not how he'd practiced in in his mind but it was absolutely perfect. I was thrilled to say yes and now we've officially started our life together. It has been hard for him to come around. The second time I celebrated a year sober, only my Mom showed up and it took place in a dark church basement, there were about 7 other people there and no cards or flowers this time. My husband couldn't bring himself to go. Now I'm back up to 3 years sober again and going stronger than ever.

We married in 2017 on the Chesapeake Bay. Pastor Ben came down from my Grandmom and Poppop's old church though they have both passed away now, counseled us and performed the ceremony. Sadly my father was hospitalized during the wedding and my brother Chuck was proud to walk me down the aisle. I am the last of my siblings to get married. It was a very small event, we didn't have much money to pull off anything big but at the end of the day we were married and that's all that matters. That was an eventful year for our entire family, not only because of our wedding.

Early in 2017 my stepmother was paralyzed in a car accident. After that happened I realized my Dad was facing health problems and issues with his memory because when I went to see him he was sitting at the kitchen table surrounded by post-it notes of things he was trying to remember. We all pulled together as a family and helped renovate his house so when his wife came home from the hospital it would be handicap accessible. In the end there, he could not manage to take care of her and she had to go stay with her daughter until she eventually died this year. I helped my father through the process of buying a house in Florida and he moved down there, where he is now. His memory is going and I am responsible for his assets, I funnel him money regularly and keep a tab on his spending and his healthcare from here.

A week after our wedding my family got the call that there was another accident. This time it was my little sister, Nicki. Her daughter happened to be at our house, still there visiting us from the wedding. I got a frantic call from my Mom who was scrambling across the country to get to her. At the time of her call she rattled off all kinds of issues it sounded like Nicki was facing, I could make out that she had one arm ripped off in the wreck and it sounded like she might have lost her legs, too. One of my coworkers heard the call come in and I instantly started to freak out. They packed up my things and drove me and my car home. I got to Nadia and told her what happened, it seemed like my coworkers were all affected by the accident too because they immediately took up a collection and by the next day my boss was back with an envelope containing enough money to fly my niece and I to Minnesota. We went as soon as we could make arrangements, not knowing if she would survive. I opened up a fundraiser online for Nicki and started spreading the word. We got to Minnesota to find her unconscious, Mom was there in time to get the nurses attention about her legs which she would have lost if Mom didn't see the signs of compartment syndrome. They were broken in a hundred places and put together with pins and rods. She had a small piece of her arm left, wrapped in bandages just below the shoulder. Her hair was long and tangled with blood, broken glass and sticks. She had tubes in her mouth and nose and hooked up all over her body, there were cords and machines and medical wraps all over her. Nicki was a single Mom, and she worked any odd jobs she could to provide for herself and her daughter after her divorce. She would deliver newspapers overnight and that is what she was doing when she slid off the road one night in a bad rainstorm. She hit a tree at the bottom of a ditch in the woods and from the roadway no-one could see her car. She laid there trapped nearly five hours until early in the morning a policeman thought he saw skid marks on the road and turned his car around on his way to work, he says he normally wouldn't take that route but for some reason that day, he did. They had to airlift her out in a helicopter and she was in surgery for hours. My sister Megan is her identical twin and had been home at the time recovering from her own surgery. She lives in Minnesota as well, Nicki moved out there to be with her because they have an inexplicable connection to each other and can't seem to survive long when they are apart. Megan had a bad feeling and was calling Nicki all night, while the phone sat in the passenger seat just out of reach. It is a miracle that she survived at all, and that someone found her in time. My mom stayed in Minnesota taking care of Nicki, it was months before she was out of the hospital and into physical rehab. When she got out she had lost her apartment and all of her sources of income, and that fundraiser I set up had pulled in $18,000 for her to start over.

When I got back to Maryland after visiting Nicki and dropping her daughter off, I had my own set of challenges. As I held a conversation with one of my coworkers I started having a seizure, right there at the reception desk. What was strange about this one is that I lost consciousness and blacked out during the conversation but did not fall. I came out of it to her snapping her fingers in my face and clapping her hands saying "Marcia! Marcia!" I had a familiar feeling of fog and déjà vu as she started to ask me if I had a history of seizures. I remembered that feeling from all the times I fell out in my drinking days, and I knew the feeling from other times I had fallen during sobriety, including the Tramadol episode and the time I almost drowned in the tub.

That is where I began facing and getting treated for epilepsy. It wasn't a quick process, getting to the bottom of it. I don't know if I struggled to explain my experiences accurately or if I was just not blessed with good doctors but eventually I got onto the right medication that would control the seizures and I stopped getting the random electric jolts. I couldn't drive for 6 months and people in AA took me to my doctors appointments and meetings, and I rode to work with my husband every day. I stayed sober through it all, and felt as if I was being tested, at times.

We waited to take our honeymoon until our first year wedding anniversary and traveled to a beautiful beach in Barbados for 2 weeks. That is when we found our mutual love of exotic beaches and are planning our next trip to go somewhere else again as soon as we can.

At the end of 2017 my husband's role on the project was up and he was sent to a power plant project here in Pennsylvania. I, however, still had a few months left on the project in Maryland and was alone for three months after he got transferred. I needed to stay and help close out the project and was one of the last people in the office to leave the construction site. I was given a healthy severance package at the end and then moved our household to Pennsylvania to be with Christian again. Of course, my Mother turned up to help us move. We have been here in Pennsylvania now for 6 months together and Christian has just been notified he is being transferred to Denver to start on a highway construction project there. We are making our arrangements to move and Mom is back, helping us get packed and ready to go. I never did find a job this last 6 months, though

I still pulled some freelance design work throughout my time here. I have been sober over 3 years and though that's not typically considered long term sobriety, in this town, it is. We are in New Castle, PA between Pittsburgh and lake Eerie and it is a small, sad town with a serious drugs and alcohol problem and not much opportunity. We both have more sobriety than most of the people in meetings here and there is one place in town where they are all held. There is a women's halfway house up the hill from the one church and every time we go to a meeting, women come trudging down the hill, 17 of them all together, and go into the meetings. I have become known at that halfway house and have had 3 sponsees there at all times. They do not all stay sober and so there has been a rotation in who I'm working with. A woman can only sponsor a limited number of people there at a time. In order for me to sponsor someone, I had to take the time with each of them and go in and meet with their counselor during the work day and talk about their recovery plan. I go in and sign out each girl and we go to my house and read the Big Book and work the 12 steps. It consumes all of my time and if this town was any better off I would have probably been able to find a job but as it sits, I seem to be needed in a different way by my Higher Power right now.

My husband and I went to the local intergroup and picked up AA service positions when we moved here. Service work is considered a very important part of AA and we generally each always keep one or two roles. His favorite thing to do is H&I, that is Hospitals and Institutions, and he takes meetings into jails and rehabs. The job that was open for me was literature rep, and I am responsible for handing out and keeping stocked all the AA literature around town. I have dropped off stacks in the libraries, some restaurants and even liquor stores, and the various places that host AA meetings. I ran across an opportunity one day at the parole & probation office in the small downtown area of New Castle, and from there became the person who speaks at DUI classes where people go who get into trouble drinking and driving. I get up in front of the classroom and tell those people my story. Whether they identify as alcoholics or not, they are required to attend these classes as punishment. How strange I walked in the door with literature at the very moment they were discussing the need for someone to come in and speak.

Marcia, Age 41

Denver, Colorado, 2022

We moved to Denver with no place to go and stayed in an air bnb for a week. During that week, our belongings were on their way across the country in a pod and we needed to find a rental quickly and give them the address of where to drop it off. We ended up with a cute little house and a big yard for way too much money. My Mom was with us and helped us move in. I haven't brought this up yet but back in Baltimore that oldtimer did end up giving me a piano and we have moved it around with us 7 times already, and I still play. I am also still a vegetarian!

We got hooked up with the local AAs here and eventually fell in with a group of friends. We had to start over again with a new homegroup, sponsor and service commitment but it's getting to be comfortable for us both to do that. One of the beautiful things about Colorado is the weather, it is sunny 300 days out of the year and there is no humidity. It is beautiful here. Christian is a snowboarder and used to teach lessons in the Poconos in his younger years. Living this close to the Rocky Mountains has given us the chance to go to the different ski resorts a lot. I am a skier, I learned in Bethesda all those years ago, and I enjoy cruising the pillow-soft snow they have out here. I prefer the easier, less challenging hills but even those runs are nearly 3 miles long. It has been one of our favorite activities. When we drove across country to move here to Denver, Christian and I both had fairly new Chevy's and a vintage Ford Bronco that we liked to take to car shows and cruise around in. He was given a work truck by the company and is a carpenter foreman in very high standing. They trust him to make decisions with million dollar equipment and he runs his own crew of workers. For a while there we had a fleet of vehicles, with his work truck, our Chevys and the Bronco.

I started applying for jobs at the same project and got a good position with placement in the office. Even though we've worked together for much of this time, we never ran into each other at work. After renting for a little while in Denver we started to look into buying a house. Such a big step felt way out of our reach, but Christian had been saving money and together we were able to pull it off. We became homeowners in 2019, living less than a mile from our workplace. It is a beautiful location and we instantly became close friends with our neighbors. We still have our goldendoodle, Aurora, and it was funny when we moved to Colorado and saw that the town next to Denver is called Aurora, I call that a God-wink. We also have a fluffy gray cat who we got together in 2017 because on top of everything that year, my old cat even died. The neighbors have goldendoodles and we put a small pet gate in the fence out back, and all the dogs would run back and forth. The cat loves going outside and any day can be spotted on our fence watching the dogs go by. Things changed drastically with the world when the great pandemic struck and our office went online. I was able to work from home through the worst of it and Christian's construction work never missed a beat. In April of 2020, his brother overdosed on heroine and died. I haven't shared much of my husband's story but he, in the past, would use with his oldest brother back in Pennsylvania. He was never able to stop, even though he kept trying. Matt was a father and left his wife and child behind, along with two stepchildren. We had to go back to Pennsylvania for the funeral and during the silence of the early pandemic time, we struggled to find a way to get there. It was a difficult time for us and Christian's side of the family and we had to lean on our friends in AA to get through it. It isn't something we will ever get over and if there is one thing I've learned through all of this, it is that tragedy isn't something you get over but something you learn to live with.

My husband celebrated 10 years sober last summer, I threw him a big party and tons of people came to celebrate with him. We have both crossed over into our forties now and are really starting to grow in our marriage. We've come through many exciting times as well as challenges and stayed together. When my husband has any spare time, he builds things. Renovates, remodels, constructs, he is always building something. When he is relaxing, he watches shows about building stuff and that is how we ended up with a beach house. He said to me one day "what do you think of this house?" Now we own a rental property at the beach in Alabama of all places because he saw it on one of those building stuff tv shows he watches. We also have a rental property in Minnesota now, that one of my younger sisters lives in. I wonder sometimes where we get the money to do the things we are doing because it seems like only yesterday when we only had twenty bucks for a week of groceries.

I was able to be there for my older brother Brian last year when he left Alaska after living there for 20 years. He moved here to Colorado and worked at the same project as my husband and I, before relocating to Minnesota and buying a house of his own. Reconnecting with Brian and getting to know his children filled my heart with joy, because after he moved and all of the issues I had, we lost touch for many years, only catching up once in a while. I helped him get settled with his kids, and was impressed to find out what a good Dad he had become. We got to play our guitars and sing together, like we used to in high school. I see that year that he lived close by as a gift, and cherish the memories we made before he moved again.

Through the last couple of years it has been hard to see my Father deteriorate in mind and in body. He had to leave Florida and go back to Maryland where we all helped get him stabilized on my brother Chuck's property. Eventually his health took a turn and he had to be hospitalized and never made it back out again. I flew home to Baltimore every couple of months when he was in the nursing home to see him, and I always sent grocery orders full of snacks to his facility. As we all started buying houses, my siblings and I, we sent him the home inspection reports to review from the nursing home and he would act like we kept him too busy, reviewing those things for us. I went out there for Father's Day in 2022 and saw him one last time. He was gone by early July. I put together an online funeral and sent the information around, and old Pastor Ben lead the service at Chuckie's house. In the end my father begged me all the time to get him out of there and take him back to Florida. He could not walk or sit up and was dying from cancer. He apologized a few times to me for not being there through my teen years, and told me he wished he had done things differently. After he was gone I had him cremated and in October went to Florida with my Mom, sister and husband and laid him to rest, scattering his ashes on the beach. I took some sand from that beach in Florida and scattered it at my beach house in Alabama and that is where I go when I need to talk to him. In the years of being sober I have learned that I am very fortunate to have always known I was loved by my father. Throughout my life, he has always played a role and I never once questioned if I was important in his eyes.

When my mother decided it was time to leave Baltimore I went out to help her pack, and when she sold that old rowhome my husband and I loaded up her things and drove it out to Minnesota where she will be able to retire close to my other 3 siblings. It is ironic, that right now she is living in my house there with my sister, looking for one to buy. She helped us with every move, that was 3 times in Baltimore, twice in southern Maryland, once to Pennsylvania and twice in Denver. Then when we finally bought a house she thought she was done, and we bought that beach house next. She has been to the beach house already and loves it about as much as we do. My Mom is everyone's champion and I think she is the hero in my story. She has never stopped being a Mom and spends her retirement going from kid to kid, helping them with their lives. I wonder sometimes if she would have been different if she did not lose her own mother, and think about the great loss she has suffered. She has always had a positive outlook and unfailing kindness, always has made the littlest things seem special. She is a unique and wonderful woman and I thank God for giving me a Mom like her.

At times I get the feeling I should speak up about my accident and will mention it in a meeting but for the most part I keep it quiet. I have shared the story at the podium many times in AA as part of service work because I was told to always say yes when asked to speak at an AA meeting or event. I am willing to talk about it when the subject comes up and I have been able to forgive myself for it, that has not wavered ever since I returned from the Ocean City trip. I was never able to make a connection with the victim's family after they took a restraining order out on me in 2001. As far as I know from reports other people have made, they are still angry and I wish I could help heal their pain, it is a major regret for me. I think about my accident at times when I am learning about my own grandmother, Gladys, and her murder. How my mother tried in vain to keep the family history of alcoholism hidden, how I tried to keep my secret hidden, how Gladys kept her abuse hidden. The word Alcoholic is not a bad word, and there is no shame in having alcoholism. I am fortunate to have found recovery and a way up and out of that misery. Many alcoholics never get the help they need and it does look a lot like depression. I think of the times in my life when I was misdiagnosed with depression when all along it was untreated alcoholism and there is a solution for that. I am grateful every single day and I ask God to help me stay sober every morning and thank God for keeping me sober every night. I thank my Higher Power for the long list of blessings I've received, the people, places and things in my life that make my existence whole. I have faith that my Higher Power has a plan for me, I recognize that I have no idea what it is. I have been shown grace and found redemption.

Writing Experience and Follow-up

Marcia, Age 41

Gulf Shores, Alabama, January 2023

I am 41 years old, I'm coming up on 8 years sober. I recently came to a cross road in life and have been facing some health issues, I needed to take some time off work to get it straightened out. During that time, I kept getting hints from my Higher Power to write my story down. I would have dreams about Gladys, or my Mother would open up about something she'd never discussed before, I even met a best-selling author in AA. I started seeing signs all over the place, so I looked into some writing classes and found a course online. Like in my school years, I breezed through it and didn't take any notes, and I'm not sure how I will title this or get it published yet at this point. My life is very full and I had a lot of exciting, but loud, things happening in Denver and our little beach rental property happened to have a cancellation that opened up over a month of availability. I decided to take my laptop and keyboard to Alabama and see where it lead. As soon as I got dropped off I placed a grocery order and locked myself inside. I have been to the beach most days as I write and research and I can see the waves through the window which I am facing. I started calling family members I haven't spoken with in years, I called some people I've never met. Everyone dropped what they were doing and told me everything they knew, it's as if Gladys cleared a path and her story began to unfold. People sent me old photos and newspaper articles. I found out that Gladys's story was used later in North Carolina to help create laws to protect battered women. I swallowed many tears, took brakes to make room for my emotions, and hit a lot of AA meetings through the process. Within two weeks I had everything complete. Last night, after my last sentence about not knowing God's plan for me, I looked at the clock and it was 6:30pm, I was done. I felt a strong urge to get to a meeting and pulled out my phone numbers I'd gotten from the women in AA my first day here. The last meeting of the night in this town started at 7pm and none of those women would have time to get here and pick me up, so I booked an Uber real quick and changed out of my sweatpants. When the car arrived, it was my dream car that I can't afford yet, and I was excited to go for a ride in it. I'll mention quickly that I have always held a love of cars, through it all, I've been interested in vintage, antique and luxury cars and am always paying attention to what the industry is doing with new vehicles, funny that my Grandad worked at Chrysler and my father took me to car shows ever since I can remember. I happened to view it as a sign. I told the driver I loved his car, a friendly young man who looked pretty well put together. We talked about writing books and I gave him the brief play-by-play of my story and when I finished my summary he was crying. He put his hands up and looked up and said "OK God! I hear you!" He told me he was a sober member of Narcotics Anonymous and that he was in the middle of a relapse, he just had to lie to his mother and his ex-wife that night to get money for drugs. He said his Higher Power was speaking to him through me and that he needed to get back into the rooms but just couldn't stop. I told him he was dropping me off at a meeting and he shook his head and said he wasn't ready to go in. As he stopped the car, someone outside recognized him, came to say hello and asked if he was coming in but all he said was that he was dropping someone off. I told him to come back when he's ready, we would save him a seat.

It feels like God is always up to something in my life and the lives of others. I use the words God and Higher Power or sometimes Universe and I think I am praying to the same God everyone else in this world prays to, I think God just looks different to all of us. I know enough to know I don't know what's going on here, but it seems like I must be on the right track. May your God bless you and keep you, until we meet on the road to happy destiny.

Marcia, Age 43

Tampa Bay Area, Florida, April 2024

It has been over a year since I finished my story. I thought I would find a way to publish it when I was ready, and have just not gotten there yet. Now, I realize I may never be ready but lately a few people have told me to 'just do it anyway.' I do not have any great accomplishments or any special happy ending to add, my career hasn't really taken off yet, I haven't made any major contributions to society, the greatest thing I have done with my life so far is stay sober and help others get and stay sober. I am a good daughter, sister, wife and friend. I continue to help as many people as I can, and have no idea who or how many I have significantly impacted, and most likely never will. Still, maybe that is enough.

Last spring my husband was offered a staff position on a large highway construction project in Fort Worth, Texas for the same company he has been a union foreman with this last decade. We had already declined a few jobs in Texas throughout the years, but felt maybe there was some reason for us to go there and went ahead with it. We moved to Fort Worth in the early summer of 2023, leaving Denver on a cool morning with all our pets and belongings in a Uhaul and a couple of vehicles in tow. By the time we got to Texas, it was hot and sunny and 115 degrees outside. The house had no electricity because I negligently set it up wrong and the neighbors came right over with a generator and fans to cool us off. Fortunately, we were able to sell our house in Denver quickly and buy one in Texas just as fast, and had a fairly smooth transition in getting settled. Real estate is complicated, but we are getting the hang of it by now, and upgraded to a huge house with a pool. Of course before we could unpack, my husband was busy tearing up the floors and renovating the whole downstairs. He insisted on making these upgrades before he had to start the new project. While we were at it, we got all new smart appliances, because one interesting thing about buying a home in Texas is they don't come with a refrigerator or washer and dryer!

That first week we went to the local AA clubhouse which held a few meetings a day. We were invited to a 'covered dish' that Saturday night before the meeting, where they celebrate what they call 'birthday night.' This birthday night came to be one of our favorite monthly occasions, however the first one was a little wild. Everyone brought a dish and the club had dinner together for an hour before the meeting, if they had just called it a 'potluck' I would have known what they meant! There was cheering and hollering and clapping, laughter, tears, making fun of each other on the microphone as people picked up their chips to celebrate various lengths of sobriety time. Christian picked up his 11 year chip that night. It was a blast, we fell in love with those good folks in Texas, they welcomed us with open arms, invited us to absolutely everything, and were serious about recovery. This group had 3 different detox facility commitments and was always looking for someone to come along, so both of us got involved pretty quickly in carrying meetings into the various hospitals and rehab places around Fort Worth.

Christian signed up for the prison commitment and finally got approved about a month before we left town. In order to go into a high security facility like a prison, you need to fill out an application and be approved before going inside. He got a new sponsor in town who was the area AA prison meeting rep and they would go together taking meetings into a place I'd be too terrified to ever re-enter. I started looking for a new job, thinking we would be in Texas for possibly 8 years if we stayed for the whole project. After multiple interviews with many different types of companies, I still never found anything for work. One night during the 'covered dish' before the birthday night meeting, someone showed me a text message saying that the company she worked for as a home health care aide needed a temp to come help in the office asap, for about 2 weeks. I took down the number and was hired by text and started the next day! This job I took as a temp was in IT, I was the tech support person responsible for migrating the business and all their clients to a new online content management system and I quickly learned how to use it and started teaching everyone else there how to implement the different features. This company was a small female-black-owned-business, I was working on site with about 15 – 20 other people and I was the only white woman there at first. I had a little bit of trauma surrounding black women after my time in prison and for some reason that started to get re-written on my soul. I really was accepted, respected and treated well by all my coworkers there. We all had a mutual respect for each other and I got to know many of them and hold them very dearly because of that experience. The owner of this company was a remarkable woman who I strive to be like, and I was instantly impressed with all of her accomplishments. I got to experience working in the home healthcare industry a little by working there, as we were the support behind hundreds of small businesses that connected home health aides with disabled people. This role that was supposed to last 2 weeks ended up going for 4 months, and I only left because my husband's job took us off to another state, yet again.

In the spring of 2024, my husband was offered a role in Florida with a different large construction company as a staff superintendent. This was such a big opportunity that we decided to go with it, even though we had only just moved to Texas. This new job would keep us in one location for good, the need to move every few years being eliminated. By the time we left Texas 7 months later, I had walked 4 women through the 12 steps out by that pool in our Texan back yard and had made some lifetime friends who I will never forget. We were very fortunate there, had wonderful neighbors and a solid AA community who showed up to help us move. Guess who else showed up for the move to Florida? My Mom came into town and stayed with us for a month while we transitioned from Texas to Florida. We put our house on the market and it sold the first day, probably because of those new floors and smart appliances my husband insisted on getting! At the same time as selling one house we were buying another and somehow the timelines worked out so that we would be able to have a place to move into when we got to the new town. Now we are in a smaller place with a little vintage pool out back surrounded by palm trees and lizards. We are within an hour's drive of so many different beaches I can't count them all. I have always loved the beach and it is almost like a dream come true that there are so many close by.

As soon as we got to Florida we hit a local meeting and started getting phone numbers of the people here in AA. I heard about a Sunday morning meeting on the beach and went that first weekend in town which happened to be my 9 year anniversary, I was able to pickup my chip on the beach. It felt like a new page was being turned in my life story that day. When we were leaving Denver I re-gifted my piano to a single Mom in need, hoping to one day fulfill my dream of getting a baby grand. Once we moved into this new place, the piano was the only thing missing and my husband found me one that is over a hundred years old and sounds like heaven when played, which is now in our living room and I can play it any time I want. Sometimes I play that baby grand piano and it takes me back to all those moments in early sobriety that only playing a piano could have gotten me through, it has always been a source of healing for me. There have been moments here when I've thought of my Dad and just wished our time could have overlapped, I think he sends little reminders that he's with me in spirit. Now that I am settled here I am looking for work again, and I can not help but wonder what the 'big guy' has in store for me next.

IV

Part Four: News

In the Media

Engineer Accused In Wife's Killing

Charlotte police Wednesday arrested a 50-year-old civil engineer for Mecklenburg County and charged him with the Wednesday morning shooting death of his wife.

County police and city police detectives arrested L e o n a r d James Hill of 722 Manhasset St. in a wooded area near Arrowood Industrial Park en hours after the body of his wife was discovered in their home.

Police said the victim, Gladys Hill, 36, was found shortly after 11 a. m. in a back bedroom of their one-story brick home.

She had been shot once in the chest and once in the jaw with a small caliber pistol.

The suspect's mother, Dawson Hill, who had lived with the couple, said her son and his wife had been separated since Feb. 5.

She said that Mrs. Hill ca...

that Hill had threatened suicide earlier and were afraid he would take his life before they could find him.

His car was spotted in the Arrowood Industrial Park by a co-worker who later saw Hill walking in nearby woods.

Five county policemen...

Guilty, Plea Is Entered In Slaying

Leonard James Hill, 50, of 722 Manhasset Rd., pleaded guilty yesterday to second degree murder in the shooting death of his wife Feb. 24.

He was placed in custody to await sentencing later this week by Superior Court Judge Harry C. Martin.

Hill first was tried last month for first-degree murder in his wife's death but a mistrial was declared. Eleven jurors voted for conviction then with just one voting for acquittal.

Police arrested Hill, who was an engineer for the Mecklenburg County Public Works Department the same day the body of his wife, Mrs. Gladys Curs Hill, 36, was found in a back bedroom of the couple's home.

Her body had two pistol wounds, one in the chest and one in the jaw.

The couple had been separated since Feb. 5 and Mrs. Hill had custody of their four-year-old son.

Mistrial Declared In Murder Case

A hung jury resulted in the mistrial yesterday of Leonard James Hill, who is charged with first degree murder.

After deliberating n e a r l y eight hours on the fate of Hill, 50, of 722 Manhasset St., the jury said it was hung on a vote of 11 to 1.

A new trial was scheduled for Dec. 13.

Hill is charged with murder in the shooting death of his wife, Mrs. Gladys Hill, 36, in the couple's home last Feb. 24.

Mrs. Hill was shot in the head and the chest. Her body was found in her daughter's bedroom.

MISTRIAL DECL...

1st-Degre...

By NANCY BRACHEY
Observer Staff writer

A mistrial was declared Monday in the first-degree murder trial of a Charlotte man after the jury reported it was hung on a vote of 11 to 1.

The Superior Court jury, who sat deliberate nearly eight hours, said it would be impossible for them to get a unanimous verdict.

A new trial was scheduled Dec. 13 for Leonard James Hill, 50, of 722 Manhasset St., on the charge of killing his wife.

Mrs. Gladys Hill, 36, was shot in the head and chest and her body found in her young daughter's bedroom at the couple's home last Feb. 24.

Assistant County Solicitor...

Pe...
pr...
ly...
tha...
cla...
tale...
wip...
sha...

He...
wan...
cont...
Mrs...
rum...

A s...
Both...
says...
pack...
said...
said I would kill my wife I would."

Mrs. Hill had been staying at Mrs. Morris' house since leaving her husband two weeks before. She had returned to the Manhasset Street house for her clothing and possessions on the morning of her death.

...right to the car to pack belongings, Mrs. Morris said she saw Hill come out of the house, charge the license plates on his automobile, and drive away. She said he waved at her.

Another police officer, C. L. Kuchenbod, testified that he went to the Hill house five days before and was requested by Hill's elderly mother to un-

...cheduled

...load a .22-caliber pistol. It was unloaded and placed in a drawer, he said.

Mrs. Hill was killed with .25-caliber bullets.

Hill testified that he did not kill his wife and had wanted a reconciliation with her.

He said he was helping his wife pack when she pulled out some weapons, held them on him and threw car keys in his face. While he was picking up the car keys he said, his wife pulled a gun on him.

He said there was a struggle over the pistol and that he didn't know when it fired. He cause his wife pushed him down and he left the room. He said the gun was not in his hands.

Neither weapons nor a gun were found by the police.

1971

THE STAR DEMOCRAT

Thursday, January 10, 2002. Page **7A**

Elkton woman's homicide trial under way

- Charged with vehicular homicide

By CARL HAMILTON
Special from The Cecil Whig

ELKTON — A trial began Tuesday for an Elkton woman accused of killing a Delaware man in a hit-and-run accident in Ocean City during Memorial Day weekend.

Marcia Beth Horn, 20, is charged with vehicular homicide, driving while intoxicated or under the influence of alcohol, failure to remain at the scene of a traffic accident involving bodily injury and other counts.

The trial is being held in Worcester County Circuit Court in Snow Hill, and it is expected to last two days. Horn's blood-alcohol level shortly after the fatal accident was .17. In Maryland, a motorist with a blood-alcohol level of .10 or greater is considered to be drunk.

Meanwhile, the blood-alcohol level of the victim, Alexander Alvarez, 23, of Bear, Del., was .28, which, had he been driving, is nearly three times higher than the legal limit.

According to police, Horn was driving her 1989 Honda Civic south on Coastal Highway about 2:30 a.m. May 26 when she struck Alvarez, who was standing about four feet into the bus lane while hailing

a cab.

The impact knocked Alvarez out of his shoes and threw his body 76 feet, police said. Prior to the accident, witnesses saw Alvarez jumping in the bus lane of the highway and, at times, making his way into the third traffic lane, according to police. Alvarez and his college friends were in the resort town celebrating his upcoming 24th birthday, police reported.

Alvarez graduated from Boston College in 1999, and he

was employed by the Hallmark Card Company. Horn allegedly continued driving south after striking Alvarez with her car, which sustained noticeable damage, including a broken windshield, police said.

An undercover detective arrested her about 20 minutes later in the parking lot of the 45th Street Village, where she attempted to flee from the officer in her car, police reported.

Prosecution rests in drunken driving trial

- Elkton woman charged in hit-and-run death of tourist on Coastal Highway in OC

Woman convicted in OC highway death

By Anita Ferguson
Daily Times Staff Writer

Judge orders woman convicted in DUI death be moved to county jail

- State's attorney's m...

THE STAR

Elkton woman found guilty

- Charged with fatal hit-and-run in Ocean City

Woman accused in fatal hit, run in O.C.

By CARL HAMILTON
Special from The Cecil Whig

2001

123

About the Author

First time author Marcia B. Horn tells the true story of HER FAMILY TREE in this first edition, three-part piece, covering her story along with the life of her Mother and Grandmother. The threads that bind these women's stories together are that of tragedy, hope, survival, redemption, love, spirituality and perseverance. Marcia writes about her life as she moves around the United States and some of her experiences with alcoholism, incarceration, recovery, PTSD and survivor's guilt. A member of the recovery community, she is looking back into some of the darkness of her past and using those tragedies to help others find sobriety.

You can connect with me on:

🌐 https://www.author-marcia-horn.com

🅵 https://www.facebook.com/author.marciahorn

Made in the USA
Columbia, SC
11 May 2024

35557053R00079